*pathfinder® guide*

D1081477

# Yorkshire Dales

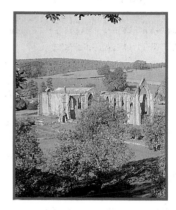

WALKS

*Originally compiled by*
*Brian Conduit*
*Fully revised by*
*Terry Marsh*

JARROLD
publishing

Acknowledgements
The author would like to thank Mr R. J. Harvey (National Park Officer)
and Mr S. Hounsham for looking at the manuscript and giving me much
useful advice. The publisher would like to thank the Yorkshire Dales
National Park Authority for its kind assistance.

Text:               Brian Conduit
                    Revised by Terry Marsh
Photography:        Brian Conduit, Terry Marsh
                    and Jarrold Publishing
Editorial:          Ark Creative, Norwich
Design:             Ark Creative, Norwich
Series Consultant:  Brian Conduit

Jarrold Publishing    ISBN 0-7117-0516-X

First published 1989 by Jarrold Publishing
Revised and reprinted 1990, 1991, 1993, 1995, 1997, 1999, 2002,
2004, 2005.

Printed in Singapore
by Craft Print International Limited. 10/05

Jarrold Publishing
Pathfinder Guides, Whitefriars, Norwich NR3 1JR
email: info@totalwalking.co.uk
www.totalwalking.co.uk

**Front cover:** The village of Muker, in Swaledale
**Previous page:** The ruins of Bolton Abbey

# Contents

The National Parks and Countryside Recreation; The National Trust; Walkers and the Law; Countryside Access Charter; The Ramblers' Association; Safety on the Hills; Useful Organisations; Ordnance Survey Maps

Short, easy walks

Walks of modest length, likely to involve some modest uphill walking

More challenging walks which may be longer and/or over more rugged terrain, often with some stiff climbs

# Keymap

Kelleth · Newbigging-on-Lune · Ash Fell · Nine Standards Rigg · Stonesdale Moor · Pennine Way · Rogan's

Bowderdale · Ravenstonedale · A683 · 1264 · B6270 · Ravenseat · West Stonesdale · Keld · 2203

West Fell · Weasdale · Pendragon Castle · B6259 · Outhgill · Birkdale Common · Angram · Thwaite · Muker

Ravenstonedale Common · 1712 · Adamthwaite · Low Dovengill · Fell End · Angram Common · Great Shunner Fell · 2349 · 2213 · SWA

HOWGILL FELLS · 1925 · 1624 · Uldale Ho · Mallerstang Common · Abbotside Common · Cotterdale · Abbotside Common

The Calf · 2219 · Low Haygarth · High Wardses · Grisedale · 25 · High Shaw

Brant Fell · Cautley · West Baugh Fell · BAUGH FELL · Garsdale Head · A684 · Hardraw · Appersett · Hawes · 2 · edbusk · W

SEDBERGH · A683 · East Baugh Fell · Grisedale · Mossdale Moor · Gayle · Burtersett · 10

19 · West Mostard · A684 · 2217 · Garsdale · 1825 · Widdale Fell · B6255 · High Houses · Wether Fell · 2015 · Marsett

Gawthrop · Dent · Rise Hill · Cowgill · 2205 · Wold Fell · 1773 · Dodd Fell · 2192 · Cragdale · LANGST

Calf Top · 1999 · 8 · Deepdale · Stone House · 1829 · Gayle Moor · Cam Fell · Oughtershaw · Beckermonds · 2109 · Tongue

Crag Hill · 2250 · WHERNSIDE · 2416 · Blea Moor · Cam Fell · Plover Hill · Halton Gill · 2001

Bullpot Farm · Leck Fell · 2057 · Ribblehead · 15 · Far Gearstones · Sike Moor · 1966 · Yockenthwaite · Hubberholme

Scales Moor · Chapel-le-Dale · B6255 · Roman Road · Selside · High Birkwith · Foxup · 18

Masongill · 2376 · Simon Fell · Horton Moor · New · Pen-y-ghent · 2231 · Litton · 2191

4 · Ingleton · Ingleborough · Newby · 27 · Moughton · Horton in Ribblesdale · Studfold · 12 · Fountains Fell · Darnbrook Fell · 1765

A687 · Burton in Lonsdale · High Bentham · Newby · 20 · Austwick · Wharfe · Helwith Bridge · Pennine Way

Mill Houses · B6480 · Keasden · Lawkland · A65 · Feizor · Stainforth · Malham Tarn

Goodber Common · Lowgill · Tatham Fells · Burn Moor · 1318 · Eldroth · Stackhouse · 21 · Langcliffe · 1815 · Kirkby Fell · 17

Thrushgill · Botton Head · 1595 · Catlow Fell · Giggleswick · Wham · Settle · Kirkby Malham · Hanlith

White Hill · 1786 · Black Hill · Cleatop · Mearbeck · Kirkby Malham · Airton · Calton

Wolfhole Crag · Long Gill · Rathmell · Long Preston · Otterburn · Pennine

1296 · 1561 · Whins Brow · Slaidburn · Ribble · A682 · Hellifield · A65 · Coniston Cold

Sykes · Dunsop Bridge · Newton · Halton West · Nappa · 719 · West Marton · East Marton · Bank Newtor

Paythorne · Newsholme · Horton

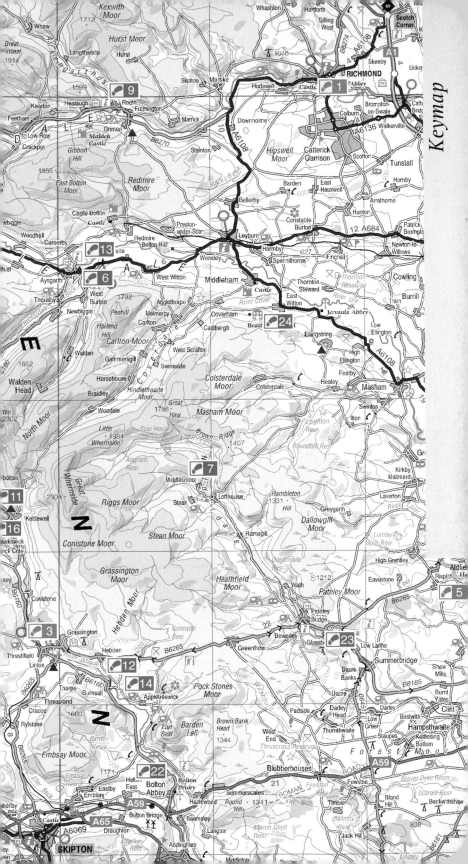

| Walk | Page | Start | Nat. Grid Reference | Distance | Time | Highest Point |
|---|---|---|---|---|---|---|
| Around Malham | 50 | Malham | SD 900627 | 7 miles (11km) | 3–4 hrs | 640ft (195m) |
| Aysgarth Falls and Bolton Castle | 39 | Aysgarth Falls | SE 012887 | 6 miles (10km) | 3–4 hrs | 690ft (610m) |
| Bolton Abbey, Barden Tower and The Strid | 67 | Bolton Abbey | SE 071539 | 7½ miles (12km) | 4 hrs | 1005ft (305m) |
| Buckden and Langstrothdale Chase | 55 | Buckden | SD 942774 | 7 miles (11km) | 3½ hrs | 1200ft (365m) |
| Burnsall and Linton | 36 | Burnsall | SE 031611 | 6½ miles (10.3km) | 3 hrs | 823ft (251m) |
| Burnsall, Trollers Gill and Appletreewick | 42 | Burnsall | SE 031611 | 7 miles (11km) | 3½ hrs | 977ft (298m) |
| Cam Head | 34 | Kettlewell | SD 968723 | 6¼ miles (10km) | 3–4 hrs | 1740ft (530m) |
| Clapham, Crummack Dale and Austwick | 61 | Clapham | SD 745692 | 7 miles (11.5km) | 3½ hrs | 835ft (255m) |
| Dentdale | 26 | Dent | SD 704871 | 6 miles (9.3km) | 3 hrs | 1165ft (355m) |
| Fountains Abbey | 20 | Fountains Abbey | SE 273687 | 5 miles (8km) | 2½ hrs | 394ft (120m) |
| Garsdale Head and Hell Gill | 76 | Garsdale Head | SD 787919 | 8 miles (12.7km) | 4–5 hrs | 1525ft (465m) |
| Giggleswick Scar and Stainforth Force | 64 | Settle | SD 819638 | 8¼ miles (13.3km) | 4–5 hrs | 985ft (300m) |
| Grassington and the River Wharfe | 16 | Grassington | SE 003638 | 5 miles (8km) | 2–3 hrs | 950ft (290m) |
| Gunnerside, Kisdon and Muker | 87 | Gunnerside | SD 951982 | 10½ miles (16.5km) | 5½ hrs | 1410ft (430m) |
| Hawes and Hardraw Force | 14 | Hawes | SD 875898 | 4 miles (6.6km) | 2 hrs | 935ft (285m) |
| How Stean Gorge and Upper Nidderdale | 24 | Lofthouse | SE 102735 | 4¼ miles (7km) | 2–3 hrs | 1000ft (305m) |
| Ingleborough | 83 | Clapham | SD 745692 | 10½ miles (17km) | 5 hrs | 1840ft (560m) |
| Ingleton Waterfalls | 18 | Ingleton | SD 695731 | 4 miles (6.4km) | 2½ hrs | 985ft (285m) |
| Jervaulx Abbey and Middleham | 73 | Jervaulx Abbey | SE 169857 | 9¼ miles (15km) | 5 hrs | 655ft (200m) |
| Kettlewell and Arncliffe | 48 | Kettlewell | SD 968723 | 6 miles (9.8km) | 4 hrs | 1607ft (490m) |
| Pateley Bridge and Brimham Rocks | 70 | Pateley Bridge | SE 157655 | 9 miles (14.5km) | 5 hrs | 950ft (290m) |
| Pen-y-ghent | 80 | Horton-in-Ribblesdale | SD 807726 | 5½ miles (9km) | 2–3 hrs | 1493ft (455m) |
| Reeth, Arkengarthdale and Grinton | 28 | Reeth | SE 039993 | 5½ miles (8.7km) | 2½ hrs | 820ft (250m) |
| Ribblehead and Chapel le Dale | 45 | Ribblehead | SD 764791 | 6¾ miles (10.8km) | 3½ hrs | 1050ft (320m) |
| Richmond and Easby | 12 | Richmond | NZ 169011 | 3½ miles (5.5km) | 2 hrs | 100ft (330m) |
| Sedbergh and Winder | 58 | Sedbergh | SD 658920 | 7 miles (11.5km) | 4 hrs | 1552ft (473m) |
| Semer Water | 31 | Bainbridge | SD 934902 | 8 miles (13km) | 4 hrs | 1739ft (530m) |
| West Burton | 22 | Aysgarth | SE 012884 | 5 miles (8km) | 2½ hrs | 755ft (230m) |

# Comments

Waterfalls, limestone gorges and the magnificence of Malham Cove combine to make this an outstanding walk, one of the finest in England.

Apart from wandering some delectable countryside, the main interests in this walk lie in the spectacular waterfalls and the dominating presence of Bolton Castle.

This walk begins across moorland pasture before descending to savour one of the most delectable stretches of the River Wharfe on its return to the ruins of Bolton Priory.

A high level outward route with superb views of Upper Wharfedale is followed by a lovely return stretch by the river, and visiting the hamlet of Hubberholme.

Starting along the river, this walk visits some stunning scenery and an isolated village before returning at a high level across undulating pastures with excellent views of the dale.

This walk combines attractive villages, open moorland, a steep-sided ravine and riverside pastures; there is also the option to visit the grounds of an outstanding 17th-century hall.

A steady climb above Wharfedale from the village of Kettlewell, the walk enjoys fine views and concludes along a section of the Dales Way beside the River Wharfe.

A fascinating encounter with glacial rubbish leads into a wild and remote dale before returning along a walled lane to the village of Austwick.

Dentdale is different from most of the dales, with hedgerows, not walls, separating the pastures. This walk begins up a wooded ravine, takes in a stroll above the valley and concludes in the company of the river.

A close encounter with a World Heritage Site which includes deer parks, water gardens, an ornate Victorian church, old mansion and the ruins of Fountains Abbey.

A demanding but invigorating walk involving stretches of trackless moorland. Not recommended for a day of poor visibility, but a delight in good weather.

Offering a stunning introduction to limestone escarpment and plateaux, this walk also has outstanding views of Ribblesdale, before experiencing the thrill of a fine cascade and the conclusion of a riverside path.

Limestone moorland, woodland and the company of the River Wharfe make this a memorable walk for all seasons.

A delightfully varied walk taking both high and low level views of Swaledale, and passing riverside meadows, moorland fringes, waterfalls and woodland.

Providing fine views across Wensleydale, this walk also takes in the highest single drop waterfall in the Dales, accessed, conveniently some might say, through a pub.

This splendid walk first visits the dramatic How Stean Gorge before sauntering up dale to explore the course of the River Nidd.

A long but delightful walk to a superb summit with excellent views, plus a chance to visit one of England's most famous pot holes.

Delightfully wooded rocky gorges provide the setting for the two main arms of this walk, linked by a trek across hill slopes with lovely views. *The paths can be very slippery when wet or icy.*

A fine, historic walk that links an abbey and a formidable castle. The views throughout are excellent, and the final stretch in the company of the Ure as good as anything in the Dales.

The initial ascent from Kettlewell is well worth the effort and rewards with delightful views. Arncliffe is a gem of a village, and the company of the Skirfare is of the highest order.

The highlight of this walk is unquestionably Brimham Rocks, a collection of weirdly fashioned gritstone boulders, but there is much more to the walk, which is best reserved for a fine day.

A popular walk to a very distinctive summit, with an option to visit a magnificent pot hole on the way up. Part of the route follows the Pennine Way. The initial descent is steep and rocky.

An opportunity to explore Arkengarthdale, the most northerly of the Yorkshire Dales before returning in a wide loop that visits Grinton, an ancient and once important centre for the dale.

Sandwiched between two of Yorkshire 'Three Peaks' this walk makes the most of the pastoral countryside and visits the outstanding Ribblehead viaduct.

A short walk from the historical town of Richmond that visits a medieval abbey, riverside paths and the trackbed of the former valley railway.

The sleek, grassy fellsides of the Howgills provide a grand introduction to this circular tour at the north-western edge of the National Park.

Visiting a lonely lake with a grim tale to tell, the walk later climbs high onto moors across which the Romans built one of their major roads.

Beginning alongside the River Ure with its spectacular falls, the walk then climbs to a hillside chapel before trekking along a splendid grassy ridge to the village of West Burton.

# Introduction to the Yorkshire Dales

An alternative name for the Yorkshire Dales could be the Middle Pennines. To the north, extending through Cumbria, Durham and Northumberland, lies the wild and remote country of the North Pennines, while to the south, eventually merging almost imperceptibly with the Peak District, are the bare gritstone moorlands of the South Pennines. The most distinctive feature of the Yorkshire Dales, which lie between them, is the magnificent limestone landscape that encompasses a major proportion of the area, and around which the National Park is largely based.

Within that area is some of the most attractive countryside in Britain, offering infinite enjoyment and variety to those who are prepared to explore on foot. On the high, exposed moorlands, often buffeted by wind and rain, lonely, austere and dramatic countryside will be found. The valleys, however, present a striking contrast: a gentle scene with small woods, riverside meadows and neat green fields separated by miles of drystone walls, dotted with exquisite and unspoilt villages whose welcoming pubs and tearooms offer relaxation and sustenance.

It is chiefly the upper and middle reaches of the valleys of the Ribble, Aire, Wharfe, Nidd, Ure and Swale, together with their tributaries and the land between them, that form the Yorkshire Dales. The unique landscape of the region has been fashioned by the combined forces of nature and man over an immensely long time.

## The forces of nature

Millions of years ago, massive earth movements thrust the Pennines above the surrounding area and also created the series of fractures called the Craven Faults. Here the rocks on one side of the fault have been lifted high above those on the other side, which have been displaced and buried thousands of feet below. This phenomenon is best observed on Giggleswick Scar, where the line of the fault is followed by the main road from Settle to Kendal. Later, during the Ice Age, huge glaciers flowed along the valleys, deepening and straightening them and smoothing their sides. As they moved, they dropped debris of different rocks at intervals, such as the Norber Erratics overlooking Crummack Dale, a large number of dark gritstone boulders perched above the surrounding plateau of white limestone. The scouring effect of the glaciers scraped clean and exposed expanses of bare rock, while torrents of meltwater from them were responsible for carving out most of the gorges in the area, such as Gordale Scar near Malham and Trow Gill near Clapham.

Limestone is the predominant rock throughout the Dales and this gives the area its most distinctive scenic features. This is especially true of the Craven area in the south, where the compacted Great Scar limestone comes close to the surface and exhibits all the features of 'karst' scenery, named after the Karst region of Slovenia, where similar geological features are found. Prominent among these features are the great expanses of exposed rock which gleam white in the sunlight, revealed in the vertical cliffs or 'scars' and the broad horizontal terraces or 'pavements'.

It is the action of water – either streams or rainwater – that produces most of the characteristics of limestone scenery. The water absorbs carbon dioxide from the atmosphere to form a weak acid solution, which slowly dissolves the limestone. The action of rainwater can be seen to good effect on the pavement above Malham Cove, the most visited of all the limestone pavements. Here rainwater has penetrated the cracks in the rock, slowly widening and deepening them to create an almost geometric pattern of blocks (called 'clints') separated by deep grooves or channels (called 'grikes').

Water finds its way through any joints in the rocks (called sink-holes), either seeping through gently or plunging down potholes (which are wider and deeper), such as the spectacular Gaping Gill on the lower slopes of Ingleborough, or Hull Pot near the base of Pen-y-ghent. This causes one of the most spectacular features of karst scenery: streams disappearing and flowing underground to leave dry valleys on the surface. As the water penetrates, it continues to dissolve

*Middle Force, at Aysgarth*

the limestone, eventually creating a network of subterranean caverns, such as the 'show caves' near Ingleton and Clapham, and the Stump Cross Caverns between Grassington and Pateley Bridge.

Farther north, in Wensleydale and Swaledale, the Yoredale series of rocks, called after the ancient name for Wensleydale, are dominant; alternating bands of coarse shales, limestone, sandstone and millstone grit. The differences between weaker and stronger rocks have created the many waterfalls found in this northern part of the dales. Millstone grit is the hardest and most weather resistant of all these rocks and, where the softer rocks have been worn away, areas of millstone grit remain, standing boldly above the surrounding landscape, either as the major outcrops that cap the summits of the 'Three Peaks' of Ingleborough, Pen-y-ghent and Whernside, or in the form of large groups of individual boulders, like the superb collection at Brimham Rocks overlooking Nidderdale. In the far north west, in the Cumbrian section of the dales, much older Silurian slates give rise to a landscape more typical of the highlands, with smooth, steep slopes bisected by deep ravines.

## Man's influence

The Yorkshire Dales was never one of the more heavily populated areas of prehistoric Britain, and consequently remains of that period (stone circles and hillforts) are comparatively few and unimpressive. The Romans likewise left little mark on the area, but the line of a Roman road running from Ilkley to Bainbridge in Wensleydale, the principal Roman fort in the area, whose grassy ramparts still crown a hill above the village, can be traced for miles across the dales, and parts of it are now put to good purpose as a magnificent scenic footpath (see Walk 10).

Most of the settlements were originally founded during the Anglo-Saxon period, either by the Angles who settled in the region following the departure of the Romans, or by later Viking colonists, both Danish and Norse, from Scandinavia.

The Danes penetrated into the area from the east coast, moving up the Humber and Ouse and across the Vale of York, while the Norsemen came from the west. A glance at a map reveals the intermingling of typical Anglo-Saxon place name endings (*-ton, -ham, -den*) with the Scandinavian endings (*-by, -thorpe, -thwaite*), and the predominance of Norse words, such as *gill, beck, fell, crag* and *scar*, describing physical features. The word 'dale' itself comes from a Danish word meaning 'valley'.

The Norman barons who accompanied William the Conqueror's successful expedition in 1066 founded churches, created hunting grounds, such as Langstroth-dale Chase in Upper Wharfedale, and, most notably, built castles at Skipton, Middleham and Richmond to secure their rule. In their wake came the monastic orders, especially the Cistercians, who were attracted to the comparatively remote and sparsely populated Yorkshire Dales because it provided them with the isolation that was an integral part of their code. Abbeys and priories arose on sheltered riverside sites at Bolton in Wharfedale, Jervaulx in Wensleydale, Coverham in Coverdale and Easby in Swaledale. Most imposing of all was Fountains Abbey, the most complete monastic ruin in Britain, which became the wealthiest of all Cistercian monasteries. The monks were great landowners and enterprising managers, clearing forests, improving drainage and developing a thriving sheep farming industry. Such entrepreneurial skills were to sow the seeds of their future downfall at the hands of Henry VIII in the 1530s.

Scottish raids were a continual threat in the later Middle Ages, which explains why residences continued to be built as fortified strongholds, as happened at Bolton Castle in Wensleydale and Barden Tower, just upstream from Bolton Abbey. After the monasteries were dissolved their extensive estates passed into new hands and this, coupled with the removal of the Scottish threat following the union of the crowns in 1603, led to a period of unprecedented prosperity in agriculture, reflected in the extensive rebuilding of farms and manor houses.

Looking around the area today it may come as a surprise to learn that the Yorkshire Dales has a long history as an industrial as well as a farming area. Lead mining was carried on for over 1,000 years, mainly in Swaledale but also in Nidderdale and Wharfedale, and only ceased in the early years of the 20th century. Quarrying, the other major industry, has continued to the present day.

### Routes and transport
Before the construction of roads and the building of the railways, the main form of transport in the dales was by foot or on horseback, using the extensive network of 'green lanes', which are easily recognisable as broad, walled tracks. These are of varying ages and came into being for varying reasons; some may be of prehistoric origin, some were Roman trackways, some were monastic trails linking powerful landowning abbeys like Fountains with their numerous estates, and many were 'drove roads'. Nowadays they make excellent walking routes, being generally well surfaced, easy to follow, reasonably straight and fairly free from obstacles. One of the longest and most impressive sections of green lane is Mastiles Lane, which runs for over four miles (6.4km), linking the former estates of Fountains Abbey around Malham with the monastic grange at Kilnsey in Wharfedale.

Undoubtedly the most spectacular transport undertaking in the dales was the Settle–Carlisle railway, built between 1869 and 1875 as a new alternative route between London and Scotland. It runs across some of the wildest and most inhospitable terrain in the country and its construction was a prodigious feat of Victorian civil engineering. Particularly impressive are the massive stone viaducts, such as Dent Head and Ribblehead, which stride across bleak and windswept countryside. Now, with the inevitable mellowing and acceptance that the passage of time brings, these appear to be almost part of the landscape, rather than the unwelcome and unsightly intrusions they seemed to be at first.

## Plantations, reservoirs and tourists

The 20th century has added at least two new features to the landscape, both of them controversial – conifer plantations and reservoirs, the latter mainly in Upper Nidderdale. But the major impact that the last century has had on the Yorkshire Dales is the growth of mass tourism. The first tourists, apart from a few early intrepid explorers, were the Victorians, who came to view what they thought of as 'picturesque' sights: either natural wonders such as Malham Cove, Hardraw Force and Brimham Rocks, or the man-made, romantic-looking ruins of Bolton Priory and Fountains Abbey. Nowadays tourists flock into the area in ever increasing numbers for a wide variety of reasons, many of them of a recreational nature: rock climbing, potholing, canoeing, fishing, cycling or, most popular of all, walking.

## The National Park

In 1954 most of the Yorkshire Dales area became one of the ten National Parks of England and Wales. The boundaries were drawn to include, for obvious scenic and geographical reasons, a corner of south-eastern Cumbria, but Nidderdale was excluded, not, it must be emphasised, through any lack of scenic qualities, but because large parts of the upper dale were owned by water authorities and there were several reservoirs in the area.

The  National Park Authority and the communities throughout the Dales welcome more and more visitors each year, but this does have an effect on the environment. To ensure that the landscape and the way of life of its inhabitants can be enjoyed in the future, it is important to treat the Dales gently. Where possible it is best to use public transport rather than your own car to reduce pollution and congestion of the environment. Information on local bus and train services can be found at any of the seven National Park visitor centres listed on page 95. By supporting local services and businesses you will be benefiting not only the Dales communities but other visitors by ensuring that they remain open.

It is also important to understand the lifestyle in the Dales: treat the landscape with care and respect, trying not to disturb the wildlife. Remember that you may often find yourself on a path which crosses land that provides the livelihood for the local farming community, so consideration and common sense are needed to avoid unnecessary disruption and damage. It may be advisable to avoid certain moorland paths in winter or after a prolonged period of wet weather, or to follow any seasonal alternative routes provided to minimise the erosion of the walking paths.

Whether within the National Park boundaries or not, the varied and glorious scenery of the Yorkshire Dales is a paradise for walkers, offering everything from gentle lowland rambles which link attractive riverside villages, to more challenging and longer hikes across the moorland and ascents of some of the well-known peaks. The walks in this book embrace all these and illustrate both the scenic variety and the rich historic heritage of this region.

# Richmond and Easby

| | |
|---|---|
| **Start** | Richmond |
| **Distance** | 3½ miles (5.8km) |
| **Approximate time** | 1½ hours |
| **Parking** | Richmond |
| **Refreshments** | Pubs, restaurants and cafés in Richmond |
| **Ordnance Survey maps** | Landranger 92 (Barnard Castle), Explorer 304 (Darlington & Richmond) |

*This easy half-day stroll begins in the centre of Richmond, a fascinating place to explore at the end of the walk. It is nowhere difficult, with good paths alongside and through riverside meadows, and always the delightful Swale for company. The remains of Easby Abbey add considerable interest to the walk, and are easily visited.*

It is a most agreeable experience to explore the streets of Richmond, one of the great historic towns of England, a supremely attractive and photogenic old market town set beside the beautiful River Swale. Parts of the medieval walls still remain, along with the gateways and the narrow winding streets that characterise early town development. Elsewhere, there are elegant Georgian thoroughfares, a spacious if rather tilted market place, two medieval churches and the tower of a Franciscan friary. Of course, it is the great Norman castle, occupying a clifftop perch above the river and guarding the entrance to Swaledale, that so dominates the town. It was founded by Alan the Red of Brittany shortly after the Norman Conquest, and still retains part of the original 11th-century castle, known as Scotland's Hall, one of the earliest domestic buildings in the country. The remainder of the castle largely dates from the 12th century. Despite its size and air of impregnability, Richmond Castle's defences were never put to the

test, and the castle enjoyed a rather peaceful existence.

🖋 For ease of parking, the walk begins from a car park along Victoria Road. From it, head along the road towards the tourist information centre near the junction with Queen's Road (the main road, which here bears left) and King Street. At this junction go forward to pass the King's Head pub and enter a narrow street, Ryders Wynd, which leads down to Frenchgate. Turn left and soon bear right into Station Road. Shortly before the road crosses the river, leave it by branching left into a side lane **A** leading to a few houses, and there bear right onto a roughly surfaced lane that soon degenerates into a broad track.

Follow the track, which soon becomes a riverside path, leading eventually to a flight of steps up to a stile/gate giving into a field. Strike diagonally across the field, heading for another gate at the bottom end of a brief, sloping path leading above the grounds of Easby Abbey. Over a stile at

*Richmond Castle*

the top of the path, bear right on a broad track to a road junction, and there turn right to walk down to a car park adjoining Easby Abbey **B**.

Easby Abbey occupies a tranquil position beside the River Swale, and apart from the occasional Scottish raid, like Richmond Castle seems to have enjoyed a peaceful existence. A house of Premonstratensian canons, it was founded in 1155, but like so many, came to an end in 1536 during Henry VIII's Dissolution of the Monasteries. The church is the least substantial surviving part, and of it only the presbytery remains, but there are extensive remains of the domestic buildings, notably the infirmary, dormitory and refectory. The inhabitants of the abbey were canons rather than monks, and so were able to serve the local population as parish priests.

Continue past the car park, following a surfaced lane and track along the bottom edge of light woodland to reach a bridge adjoining a cottage. **C** Turn right over a bridge spanning the river, having now encroached onto the trackbed of a former railway. This leads easily back to the old railway station, passing to the left of it to a road, and soon emerging on the main road not far from Station Bridge.

Walk to the bridge, and there go down steps to the riverbank, and then turn left under the bridge and along a riverside path once more. At the next bridge **D**, Richmond Bridge, turn right and walk up Bridge Street towards the centre of town. Turn right into Cornforth Hill and at a T-junction turn right again to reach the Market Place. Across the far side of Market Place is King Street, at the far end of which you meet Victoria Road. Turn left to return to the car park. ●

# *Hawes and Hardraw Force*

| | |
|---|---|
| **Start** | Hawes |
| **Distance** | 4 miles (6.6km) |
| **Approximate time** | 2 hours |
| **Parking** | National Park station car park, Hawes |
| **Refreshments** | Pubs and cafés in Hawes and at Hardraw |
| **Ordnance Survey maps** | Landranger 98 (Wensleydale & Upper Wharfedale), Explorer OL30 (Yorkshire Dales – Northern & Central areas) |

*With the agreeable prospect of lunch in Hawes before or after the walk, this half-day excursion is a relaxing and pleasant introduction to Wensleydale. The walk includes a visit to Hardraw Force, the highest single fall in the Dales.*

Hawes is a quaint arrangement of alleyways and cottages, concealed nooks and crannies, that give the impression of mellowed old age, but the town is only a mere youngster, unable to trace its pedigree beyond the 14th century. In fact, when the *Domesday Book* was compiled, Hawes and the countryside about was forest land, and, as Camden saw it, 'a dreary waste and

SCALE 1:25000 or 2½ INCHES to 1 MILE 4CM to 1KM

0 200 400 600 800 METRES 1

0 200 400 600 800 1000 YARDS

KILOMETRES
MILES
1

horrid silent wilderness among the mountains...' The region, above and around the town, is still wild, but perceptions change and today the fellsides provide plenty of excuses to explore.

Begin from the corner of the car park on the site of the former railway and walk up a ramp to the road. Turn right to cross the railway line. Moves are afoot to re-open parts, if not all, of the railway line through Wensleydale, hopefully as far as Garsdale, where it would link with the Settle–Carlisle line.

Take the first turning on the left, which goes into a small industrial estate, but immediately abandon that by crossing a stile onto a paved section of the Pennine Way, which heads across a field to re-emerge on the road near Hayland's Bridge.

Cross Hayland's Bridge, continuing along and up the road (*take care against approaching traffic*) as far as the signposted turning for Hardrow (sic) and the Pennine Way **A**. Here leave the road, and go forward along a field-edge path. Continue by an obvious route across a series of fields to enter the village of Hardraw opposite the Green Dragon Inn.

Visitors wanting to see Hardraw Force must enter the pub and pay a small fee, as the waterfall is on private land. From the back of the inn, a path leads up into the amphitheatre into which Hardraw Beck plunges spectacularly.

Having visited the falls, turn around the end of the inn and through a gate and onto a footpath (signposted for Simonstone), which passes a cottage then soon starts heading up a field to a step-stile. Nearby, in the wall on the left, is a small mosaic, one of more than 20 placed in walls around Hawes as part of a community project to celebrate the Millennium.

*Meadowland and field barn, Hardraw*

Over the stile, climb some more to a house and outbuildings, and from it head across two fields towards the prominent Simonstone Hall Hotel, emerging onto a lane opposite the hotel entrance **B**. Turn right and walk out to a T-junction. Go left to a signposted stile on the right giving onto a footpath for Sedbusk. Initially the path goes forward as a broad track towards farm buildings, beyond which cross a ladder-stile and then pursue an obvious route across a succession of fields linked by gated gap-stiles.

Eventually, the ongoing path emerges into the hamlet of Sedbusk, opposite a telephone box. Turn right and walk down to a junction near a post box in a wall, and here turn right along a narrow lane, passing Rose Cottage. After about 165 yds (150m), leave the lane at a signposted path on the left **C** for Hayland's Bridge. Go through a gap-stile and downfield, to the right of a barn and across to another stile beyond.

The gated route leads to a road, cross this and go through another stile. In the ensuing pasture a clear, grassy path leads across to Hayland's Bridge. The path first crosses a stream by a footbridge before continuing out to meet the road. Turn left and retrace the outward route back to Hawes. ●

# Grassington and the River Wharfe

| | |
|---|---|
| **Start** | Grassington |
| **Distance** | 5 miles (8km) |
| **Approximate time** | 2–3 hours |
| **Parking** | National Park car park in Grassington (Pay and Display) |
| **Refreshments** | Pubs and cafés in Grassington |
| **Ordnance Survey maps** | Landranger 98 (Wensleydale & Upper Wharfedale), Explorer OL2 (Yorkshire Dales – Southern & Western areas) |

*Grassington, capital of Upper Wharfedale, surrounded by limestone moorland, woodland and with riverside paths radiating from it in all directions, is a walker's paradise. Not surprisingly, given the extravagant beauty of these surroundings, the Dales Way wanders through here, and part of it is used to start this walk which later turns into a woodland nature reserve before dropping to the River Wharfe for the final stage back to Grassington.*

Leave the car park and turn left and, a short way on, go right up Grassington's main street, which is lined with shops, pubs and cafés. The cobbled market square is especially attractive, as are many of the old stone houses built from the 17th to the 19th centuries. Three hundred years ago, Grassington was a small farming centre that later expanded as lead mining, textile and quarrying industries developed. Today, Grassington thrives on tourism.

Go up the main street and near the top turn left into Chapel Street **Ⓐ**. Leave the street at Bank Lane, by turning right onto the Dales Way foot-path (signposted to Kettlewell), and soon enter a walled track. Follow this until the track forks (at gates), and here leave

it by turning left through a narrow metal gate. Cross the ensuing field to a through-stile in a wall opposite. Over this, bear left, descend a short distance to a signed and gated gap-stile on the right, and after this strike across the next field to a very narrow squeeze-stile. Cross the next pasture, following a broad, grassy path to the far side of the field, where it bears left beside a wall. Pass a wall gap and locate another squeeze-stile a few strides farther on. Go through this, and head for another a short distance away, there entering Lea Green, site of ancient settlements.

Just after passing through the intake wall, the ongoing track forks. Branch left along a broad grassy track, which a short way farther on forks again. This time branch right through Lea Green

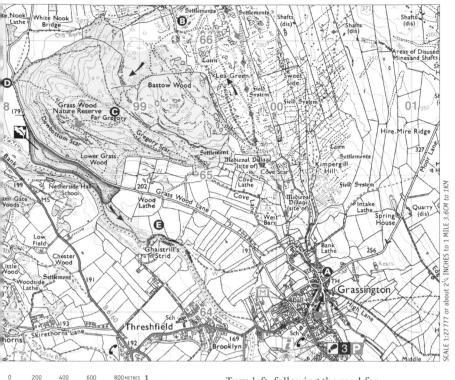

SCALE 1:27777 or about 2½ INCHES to 1 MILE 3.6CM to 1KM

| 0 | 200 | 400 | 600 | 800 METRES | 1 | |
|---|-----|-----|-----|------------|---|---|
| | | | | | | KILOMETRES |
| | | | | | | MILES |
| 0 | 200 | 400 | 600 YARDS | | ½ | |

and onto the edge of a limestone escarpment, heading towards a wall at the eastern boundary of Bastow Wood.

The path continues roughly parallel with the woodland boundary wall and eventually is joined by a grassy vehicle track from the right, immediately after which the route reaches a ladder-stile and gate **B**. Over this, go into Bastow Wood, initially keeping forward between low hills but gradually swinging round into woodland cover and pressing on to reach a ladder-stile at the edge of the Grass Wood Nature Reserve, a Woodland Trust property.

Over the stile, go forward on a clear track that leads down to intercept a broad track at a signpost **C**. Turn right (signposted for Grass Wood Lane), and follow the track, ignoring all branching paths, as it descends through the nature reserve. Eventually, the track leads down to Grass Wood Lane **D**.

Turn left, following the road for about 440 yds (400m) to a gate and stile on the right at which the road can be left for the riverside confines of Lower Grass Wood. The path descends to the left bank of the River Wharfe. After a while, the path climbs above the river, and when it forks take the right-hand branch, descending once more to the riverbank, and continuing forward, following the river to the sweeping S-bend at Ghaistrill's Strid **E**.

Head for a nearby ladder-stile, beyond which a path runs on beside a wall and above the river. Maintain the same direction, crossing four stiles and/or gates to reach a large riverside pasture. Head for a footbridge spanning an in-flowing stream, and then continue along the riverbank.

In the last field before Grassington Bridge, bear across towards the left-hand side of the bridge, where a broad track leads up to the road. Turn left and walk back up into Grassington to complete the walk. ●

# Ingleton Waterfalls

| | |
|---|---|
| **Start** | Ingleton |
| **Distance** | 4 miles (6.4km) |
| **Approximate time** | 2½ hours |
| **Parking** | Station car park, Ingleton (Pay and Display) |
| **Refreshments** | Ingleton pubs and cafés |
| **Ordnance Survey maps** | Landranger 98 (Wensleydale & Upper Wharfedale), Explorer OL2 (Yorkshire Dales – Southern & Western areas) |

*This is an 'up, across and down' walk: 'up' the narrow rocky gorge of the River Twiss, 'across' a stretch of open country, and 'down' the even rockier and narrower gorge of the River Doe. It is spectacularly attractive whatever the season or the weather, and although the paths are clear and well-surfaced,* care is needed on some stretches where the rock is slippery when wet. In freezing conditions, some of the paths are icy. *Although a short walk, there is much to see, and quite a lot of clambering up and down steps. As most of the walk is on private land, there is a nominal charge for visitors.*

Ingleton is a delightful, homely place, dominated by a huge Victorian railway viaduct, now redundant, but formerly responsible for bringing tourism to the area. Tourists still arrive in their droves, making this walk one of the most popular in the area.

🖊 Begin from the car park and walk out to the main road (or there is a flight of steps from the corner of the car park), turn right towards the village centre, and soon bear left, downhill, into a side road (signposted 'Waterfalls Walk'). At a junction, keep left to cross first the River Doe and then the River Twiss, both of which soon meet up a short way down river. After the Twiss, turn right on a side track **A** leading towards the waterfalls and a ticket kiosk.

Keep forward across a large car park,

*Thornton Force, Ingleton*

and on the far side continue along a broad track that soon narrows to a path, following the course of the River Twiss. A kissing-gate marks the start of Swilla Glen, a steep-sided river ravine, bright with flowers and loud with birdsong. Keep an eye open for the 'Money Tree' – a fallen tree now studded with coins – but do not expect to find a fortune, all the coins are bent and battered.

Onward, there is no choice of route, and a good, clear path leads to a footbridge spanning the river and on to another just below the impressive Pecca Falls. The path now climbs above the falls, with white water a constant companion as far as a seasonal snack kiosk near the top of the ascent, which also serves as a ticket sales point for anyone undertaking the walk in the opposite direction.

Go past the kiosk **B**, and soon reach the superb Thornton Force, an outstanding single drop waterfall over bedrock layers that span millions of years.

Climb past the falls, to gain a much more tranquil area, where the river is sedate and unhurried and the valley sides lean back and relax. Another footbridge leads to steps climbing out of the gorge, and onto a constructed path to a gate.

Through the gate, turn right onto a walled track, and follow this as far as a farm **C**. Go forward passing the farm, beyond which an ongoing track (signposted to Beezley Falls) leads down to a lane (Oddie's Lane).

Cross the lane and go forward onto an access track opposite. This, too, leads to a farmhouse, there swinging right to pass in front of the farm, and shortly leading to a gate giving into the wooded gorge of the River Doe **D**.

Now more waterfalls appear, beginning with the Beezley Falls. The ongoing path twists and turns, climbs

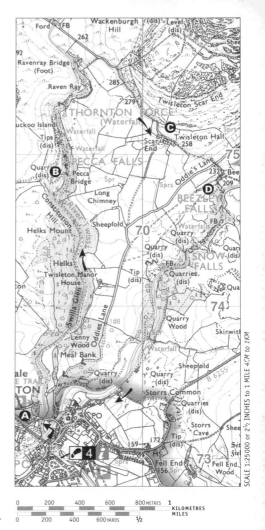

SCALE 1:25 000 or 2½ INCHES to 1 MILE 4CM to 1KM

and falls, but is never in doubt and provides a wonderful trip through the gorge: Rival Falls, Baxenghyll Gorge and the Snow Falls all provide interest and entertainment. A footbridge takes the path onto the true left bank of the river, after which the gorge widens and becomes less steep-sided.

Soon Ingleton appears ahead, as an old quarry is passed. The path broadens into a rough track that leads out to a gate, beyond which a surfaced lane leads into the village. At the main street, turn right, and follow this through the centre, and back to the station car park.

# *Fountains Abbey*

| | |
|---|---|
| **Start** | Fountains Abbey Visitor Centre |
| **Distance** | 5 miles (8km) |
| **Approximate time** | 2½ hours |
| **Parking** | Visitor centre car park (charge for admission to grounds) |
| **Refreshments** | Restaurant at visitor centre |
| **Ordnance Survey maps** | Landranger 99 (Northallerton & Ripon), Explorer 298 (Nidderdale) |

*Much of this walk falls within the boundaries of Studley Royal Country Park, a World Heritage Site owned and maintained by the National Trust and which includes Fountains Abbey. The abbey, the most complete and extensive monastic remains in Europe, is the centrepiece of the park, but is far from being the only attraction. This tour visits farmland and deer park, 18th-century water gardens and a 19th-century church, and, of course, the abbey itself. The going is gentle throughout, and the walk both relaxing and fascinating: there is an admission charge for non-Trust members.*

Go through the visitor centre and take the path ahead, turning right at a signpost to follow a curving path downhill. Bear right and head down to pass through a metal gate. When the path forks, branch right to head for Fountains Hall. Turn left and then right to pass in front of the hall, a fine mansion built in the early 17th century by Sir Richard Gresham, one of the benefactors of Henry VIII's Dissolution of the Monasteries: the hall uses stones from the abbey.

Head out of the grounds and turn left onto the road for Harrogate. Keep on the road as far as a bridleway sign on the left beside a gate and stile **A**. Over this, go forward on a broad grassy path and soon walk beside the abbey walls. Gradually, the path moves away from the wall to leave the abbey grounds at a

gate giving onto a broad, fenced track leading towards Hill House Farm.

At the end of the track, which can be very muddy after rain, bear right to a gate, and then follow an ongoing track which shortly curves left to face the front of the farmhouse. Go through a farm gate and bear right in front of open barns. At the end of the barns, the route turns left and immediately right (waymarked) and continues along the edge of a field alongside a hedgerow. Where the hedge ends, go left, downhill, to a gate near the edge of woodland. Pass through the gate onto a path through the woodland.

Descend to a track junction **B** and turn sharply left to continue down a steep-sided, wooded valley. At the bottom, cross a footbridge spanning the River Skell near a ford, turn right and

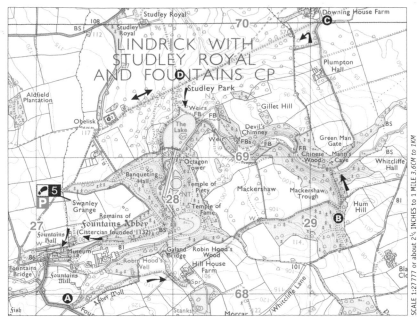

SCALE 1:27777 or about 2¼ INCHES to 1 MILE 3.6CM to 1KM

follow a broad track uphill, leaving the woods at the top of the ridge to emerge into open country. Now continue along the track towards Studley Roger. On approaching the village, the track becomes surfaced. Just before the village, turn left **C** to enter Studley Royal Country Park.

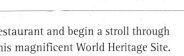

Studley Royal Country Park was created in the 16th century, but its present appearance dates mainly from 1699, when the estate came into the ownership of John Aislabie, sometime Chancellor of the Exchequer before becoming involved in the financial scandal of the South Sea Bubble over which he had to resign, even serving a brief spell in prison. On his release, he concentrated on his estates in Yorkshire, transforming part of them into a landscaped water garden.

Walk along the drive, through the elegant 18th-century gateway, into the deer park, and keep ahead to a junction of park roads **D**. The route turns left to the lakeside, but it is worth going ahead for a few hundred yards to visit the ornate Victorian church. After turning left to the lakeside, continue to the restaurant and begin a stroll through this magnificent World Heritage Site. Keep to the main path as it threads its way round small lakes, canals and cascades, past classical temples, across lawns and through woods. Finally, keep along the riverbank for the finest view of all, the abbey ruins.

Fountains Abbey was founded in 1132 by Benedictine monks from St Mary's Abbey in York. They were granted land in what was then remote wilderness by the Archbishop of York, and over the next two centuries, built up what was to be the wealthiest Cistercian monastery in England. Like other large monasteries, it was dissolved in 1539 by Henry VIII, but its comparative remoteness has ensured that its buildings have remained almost intact.

Just after passing the west front of the abbey, bear right off the main path along an uphill path through trees, and turn right through a metal gate to return to the visitor centre.

# West Burton

| | |
|---|---|
| **Start** | Aysgarth (near Yore Bridge) |
| **Distance** | 5 miles (8km) |
| **Approximate time** | 2½ hours |
| **Parking** | Aysgarth Falls car park (just before the church) |
| **Refreshments** | Pub in West Burton, pubs and cafés in Aysgarth |
| **Ordnance Survey maps** | Landranger 98 (Wensleydale & Upper Wharfedale), Explorer OL30 (Yorkshire Dales – Northern & Central areas) |

*West Burton lies near the junction of Wensleydale and the tributary valleys of Bishopdale and Walden. This modest walk begins with a stroll alongside the River Ure, then heads up to the remains of a hillside chapel before taking an exhilarating ridge walk to the lovely village of West Burton. It concludes with a little climbing before descending to Palmer Flatts and the parish church.*

Leave the car park and turn right, shortly turning into the grounds of St Andrew's Church. Pass to the right of the church and go down an enclosed pathway to a narrow gated gap-stile.

The church of St Andrew, the parish church of Aysgarth, stands on the site of a church built in the 10th century, though most of the existing church is 19th century. It is especially renowned for the Jervaulx Screen in the chancel, regarded as the best screen in Yorkshire. The vicar's desk is also quite elaborate.

From the gate cross the ensuing field, climbing easily to the edge of a small woodland, and through this bear left along a broad grassy path which shortly brings the Aysgarth Falls into view, as it runs alongside the remains of a collapsed wall. It then descends to parallel the River Ure, and soon passes the lower falls and descending to a gate in a field corner. Through this and over a stile, continue in the same direction just above the river, and eventually descend to the riverbank.

The ongoing path continues to follow the river, from time to time passing through gated gap-stiles, and finally bearing diagonally across a field to reach the valley road at Hestholme Bridge **A**. Cross the bridge and follow the road, climbing a little, for 770 yds (700m), taking care against approaching traffic, and finally leaving the road at two signposted footpaths on the right, near a farm.

Take the left-hand footpath, signposted for Templars Chapel. The path leads to a gate at the bottom of a wooded slope, and gives onto a rising stony track. At the top of the track **B**, the route turns abruptly right onto a footpath signposted for Morpeth Gate. First, take a moment to go into the adjacent field to visit the remains of the Penhill Preceptory. The continuing footpath accompanies a wall at the top

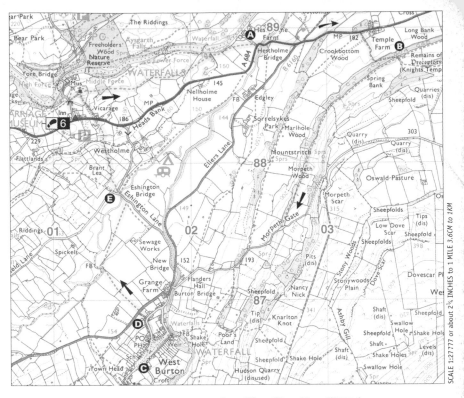

SCALE 1:27 777 or about 2¼ INCHES to 1 MILE 3.6CM to 1KM

0    200    400    600    800 METRES   **1**
                                        KILOMETRES
                                        MILES
0    200    400    600 YARDS   ½

edge of woodland, and eventually intercepts a stony track (Morpeth Gate). Now turn right, heading down the track, which ends at the road leading, left, into West Burton. Go towards the village, and shortly, as the road bends right, keep ahead for the village centre. Walk up the left-hand side of the village green, and then, at the far side (near the telephone box) **C**, circle right to come back down to pass the village shop. Just after passing the shop, bear left, heading out of the village. As the road bends to the right, leave it by turning left onto a narrow and enclosed path at the side of the Reading Room **D**, signposted for Eshington Bridge.

Steps lead down to a road. Go right and immediately left at another footpath sign, and head down-field, aiming to the left of a barn. After the barn, keep to the right of overhead powerlines, heading for a stile in the far corner of the field. Walk to another stile nearby, and from this, bear right,

shortly walking alongside a wall to a step-stile. Now cross the middle of a large pasture to reach the road near Eshington Bridge **E**.

Turn left to cross the bridge, and then bear right with the main road, but almost immediately leave it at a footpath signposted for Palmer Flatts. Walk up-field aiming for a powerline pole and another stile just beyond it. From this turn right to another gate nearby, and climb into the next field, soon bearing right to a gate. A green path, signposts and gap-stiles show the way across a complex arrangement of enclosed fields.

Eventually the path comes out onto the main valley road. Cross and go ahead along a track opposite that leads directly to St Andrew's Church. Continue to the church doors, and there turn left to return to the car park.     ●

# How Stean Gorge and Upper Nidderdale

| | |
|---|---|
| **Start** | Lofthouse |
| **Distance** | 4¼ miles (7km) |
| **Height gain** | 625ft (190m) |
| **Approximate time** | 2–3 hours |
| **Parking** | Lofthouse (limited parking) or How Stean car park |
| **Refreshments** | Café at How Stean Gorge, pubs at Middlesmoor and Lofthouse |
| **Ordnance Survey maps** | Landranger 99 (Northallerton & Ripon), Explorer OL30 (Yorkshire Dales – Northern & Central areas) |

*How Stean Beck makes an impressive display as it bullies its way through a narrow gorge bound for the River Nidd, which it joins below the village of Lofthouse. This walk probes farther into this delightful dale, reaching as far as the village of Middlesmoor, where, from its hilltop churchyard, there is a lovely view down the length of the dale into which the final section of the walk is drawn.*

This walk can begin in Lofthouse, and the route is described from there, but it goes up to pass the How Stean car park.

Opposite the post office in Lofthouse, a track runs between cottages to a footbridge spanning the River Nidd.

*Lofthouse village*

Over the river, cross to the Scar House road and a gate. Go between a barn and a playing field to another gate in a wall corner, after which the Middlesmoor road is encountered. Turn right for a few strides, then bear left onto the road for Stean, soon passing the car park and crossing How Stean Beck. Follow the road as it turns right and passes the entrance to How Stean Gorge.

There is a charge for admission to the How Stean Gorge, a narrow chasm carved through the rocks, and if time allows this should be included in the walk.

Return to the road and turn right, walking as far as a stile at a footpath signposted to Middlesmoor 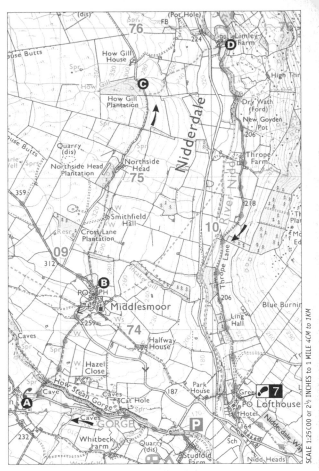 **A**. The on-going path soon crosses How Stean Beck, and ascends steps to a gate. From the gate, head for a wall gap on the right, and then turn left onto the Nidderdale Way which now leads on across fields to meet the lane into Middlesmoor.

Walk up towards the village, a lovely place perched high above the dale. The church, St Chad's, and its churchyard are well worth visiting. Go past the pub, and just after the final building on the right, turn right onto a track **B**, but turn immediately left through a gate onto a grassy path past a car park.

Cross a stile, and go forward alongside a wall (on the left) to another stile at the western edge of a narrow plantation. Keep on through a gap and tend right in the next field to yet another stile, from which the route maintains much the same direction across more fields and heading for a track that runs to Northside Head Farm.

Turn right along the track and continue beyond the farm, at first still on the track but then alongside a wall on the right to reach a gate at the edge of How Gill Plantation **C**. Here turn right and pass through another gate and start going downhill. Bear left to cross a stream and then aim for a fence/wall corner.

Cross a stile and head for the bottom left-hand corner of a field. Climb stone steps and go ahead to a stile after which head obliquely across the next field to

another stile. A short way on the Scar House road is reached **D**.

Cross the road and the field opposite to reach Limley Farm. On reaching the farm buildings turn right onto its access track, but soon leave it, on the left, as it turns up towards the valley road. Not long after leaving the farm, once more along a stretch of the Nidderdale Way, the route crosses the line of the River Nidd, which does not always have water in it.

Across the river, pursue a track known as Thrope Lane, which takes a slightly elevated course, with lovely views, to intercept a road that leads directly back to Lofthouse. ●

# Dentdale

| | |
|---|---|
| **Start** | Dent |
| **Distance** | 6 miles (9.3km) |
| **Approximate time** | 3 hours |
| **Parking** | Dent (Pay and Display) |
| **Refreshments** | Pubs and cafés in Dent |
| **Ordnance Survey maps** | Landranger 98 (Wensleydale & Upper Wharfedale), Explorer OL2 (Yorkshire Dales – Southern & Western areas) |

*Dentdale is noticeably different from the other Dales in having most of its fields separated by hedgerows rather than drystone walls, and here the practice of laying hedges still goes on, a wonderfully ecologically friendly way of fencing fields. This walk from the village of Dent begins up a narrow wooded ravine and rises to meet an ancient packhorse trail before sweeping down across hill farmland to meet the River Dee.*

The whitewashed cottages, cobbled streets, 12th-century church and splendid location just above the valley river give Dent an inspirational setting. In the 17th and 18th centuries, this was the hub of an extensive hand-knitting industry, but its most famous inhabitant was Adam Sedgwick, Woodwardian Professor of Geology at Cambridge, though one record suggests he was ignorant of matters geological and only began to study the subject on his appointment.

Leave the car park, cross into the lane opposite, and walk up past the village green. Continue in the same direction into the wooded confines of Flinter Gill, through which a stony track rises steadily. This is a former packhorse trail that climbed, as this walk does, to meet Occupation Road before heading westwards across South Lord's Land into Barbondale. At the top of the ascent a conveniently placed bench

offers a moment of retrospective contemplation – and a breather. Go through a gate to meet Occupation Road at a T-junction **Ⓐ**. Turn right, signposted for Keldishaw.

The 'Occupation Road', an ancient highway dating from 1859, sweeps south across the moorland fellsides and is a delight to amble. Do so for 1¼ miles (2km) until the track emerges onto the Barbondale road. There turn right to follow the road for 500 yds (450m), and then leave it at a signposted footpath on the left for Underwood **Ⓑ**.

Follow a broad grassy track that curves around a low hill dotted with limestone outcrops (Stone Rigg) to reach a ladder-stile. Over this, go forward alongside a dilapidated wall, but as this starts to climb the fellside above, so the track bears off to the right, and eventually curves around the shoulder of the fell and passes at a

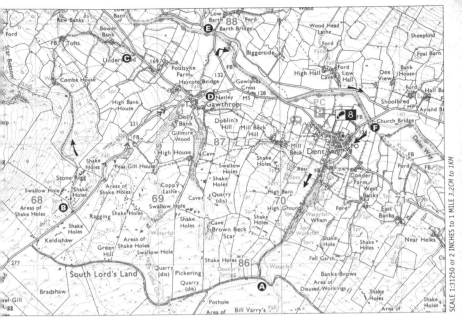

SCALE 1:31250 or 2 INCHES to 1 MILE 3.2CM to 1KM

| | | | | | |
|---|---|---|---|---|---|
| 0 | 200 | 400 | 600 | 800 METRES | 1 |

KILOMETRES
MILES

| | | | | |
|---|---|---|---|---|
| 0 | 200 | 400 | 600 YARDS | ½ |

distance below the craggy hillside of Combe Scar to reach the ruined Combe House. Go past the derelict farm and continue down a broad track that would once have been its access, to approach the farm at Tofts. Just before Tofts the track crosses a ford, but this is not the right of way, which lies a little to the left, downstream, crossing the stream by a narrow footbridge. From this climb the bank to reach a metal gate between farm buildings, and through this go forward to a wooden gate, and then follow the farm access past the small group of buildings at Bower Bank and out to meet a narrow lane **C** on the edge of Gawthrop.

Turn right and walk into and through Gawthrop, and on leaving the village also leave the road at a signposted footpath for Barth Bridge **D**. Walk past farm buildings and through a gate, and then continue alongside a fence to a low step-stile giving onto a path above a steep-sided ravine. The subsequent way down-field is well-waymarked and leads to a gated gap-stile on the left. Through this turn immediately right and continue to parallel a wall, which

becomes increasingly subdued by an overgrown hedge. This leads to a gate giving onto a road. Turn left to Barth Bridge **E**.

On the bridge, and just before the river, turn right to join the Dales Way (signposted for Hippins), which now leads all the way back to Dent. Set off across a meadow on a green footpath. The route is easy to follow, maintaining company with the river, and for a short stretch emerging onto the road before turning away again (signposted for Church Bridge). At this point, the shortest way back to the start is along the road, *but the riverside alternative is not much longer and provides lovely views of the village and its church.*

Resume the riverside path and follow this until, just after a narrow footbridge, the Dales Way goes up steps at Church Bridge to meet a road. Here **F**, turn right and walk up the road to the village, passing a large, stone memorial to Adam Sedgwick before returning to the car park.

# Reeth, Arkengarthdale and Grinton

| | |
|---|---|
| **Start** | Reeth |
| **Distance** | 5½ miles (8.7km). Shorter version 3½ miles (5.5km) |
| **Approximate time** | 2½ hours (1¾ hours for shorter version) |
| **Parking** | Village green, Reeth (voluntary contribution for parking) |
| **Refreshments** | Pubs and cafés in Reeth and pub in Grinton |
| **Ordnance Survey maps** | Landrangers 92 (Barnard Castle) and 98 (Wensleydale & Upper Wharfedale), Explorer OL30 (Yorkshire Dales – Northern & Central areas) |

*Most visitors to this corner of the Dales have arrived from east or west along Swaledale, and it is this beautiful dale that holds many people's attention. But extending northwards from Reeth is the most northerly of the dales, Arkengarthdale, a long and sinuous route into the hills. The first part of this walk investigates Arkengarthdale, while the second heads across riverside meadows to the nearby village of Grinton from where it treks across more riverside fields to a footbridge spanning the Swale and an easy return to Reeth. The contrast between the two halves is distinct and appealing: the one giving a distant view of the wild upper reaches of Arkengarthdale, the other enjoying riparian rambling of the highest order.*

Reeth was formerly an important centre for a lead mining industry, but is today an immensely popular resort for day-trippers who flock here to sample afternoon teas, locally made bread and cakes and the invigorating scenery. The village spreads itself around a green, split by the main road, and has an attractive display of cottages and houses.

🖊 From the village green, walk across to the post office and bear left to pass the Ivy Cottage Tea Room and then right towards the Arkleside Hotel. Just past the hotel, leave the road by branching left onto a signposted foot-path to a narrow gap-stile, and then across to a gate gap. In the next field, bear left to a gate and stile giving onto a farm access. Immediately turn left, and follow the access out to meet the road.

Turn right, taking care against approaching traffic, and follow the road for 550 yds (500m) to a point where the road bends left after having crossed a cattle-grid. Here, look for a signposted stile in the wall on the right (for Langthwaite) **Ⓐ**. In the ensuing field, bear slightly right, but clearly heading up-dale on a grassy path that links a long series of mainly gap-stiles.

Eventually, the ongoing path meets a field vehicle track and descends to a signpost. Here, bear right on the track (signposted for Fremmington (sic)), and go down to cross a bridge **B** spanning the river.

After the bridge, the ongoing track bears right and shortly swings left at a signpost for Fremington. It then climbs gently alongside a wall. A little higher up, the track leaves the wall and bears right, up towards a farm. Ascend to a gate to the right of the farm building, and through this cross to another gated gap-stile. Cross the next field, and then once more follow a clear grassy route across a series of walled pasture, now

*Farm cottage, Arkengarthdale*

heading back down the dale.

Continue past a derelict farmhouse and keep on to a signpost beside a pair of old gate pillars. Here, the path forks, with one path descending towards the riverside. Ignore this, and instead keep left onto a gently rising stony track along the base of lightly wooded slope.

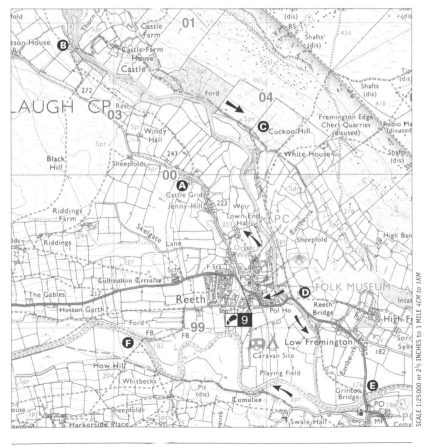

*Reeth village centre*

present church is mainly 15th century, but parts of it date to the 12th century, and it has held a key influence on the life of dales people since that time. It is a low, grey church but of considerable interest with a lovely Jacobean pulpit and a drum-shaped Norman font.

Keep an eye open for an old lime kiln in among the trees.

The path now runs above a wall. Stay on it as far as a metal gate and gap-stile **C**. A barn in the field below bears a large white double arrow. Descend to pass to the right of the barn and down to a gap-stile and cross another field to a second stile. Through this, bear left and once more follow a grassy path across walled pastures linking gap-stiles.

The ongoing path eventually leads on to the edge of Reeth and out to the main road **D**.

*The shorter version of the walk here turns right over a road bridge and soon reaches the village green in Reeth.*

For the longer walk, turn left on reaching the road, following it for about 165 yards (150m) to a signposted footpath at a kissing-gate for Grinton.

The path passes a farm, and then, as a grassy path, crosses a large riverside pasture, and then across more pastures to steps leading up onto Grinton Bridge **E**. Turn right over the bridge and walk to the village, taking the first gate giving access into the churchyard.

During the Middle Ages, Grinton, which is an older settlement than Reeth, was the only place in the dale with a church. Dedicated to St Andrew, the

Pass to the right of the church to a gate at the far side giving onto a delightful riverside path that shortly leads up steps to give onto a narrow lane.

Walk along the lane until it bends left, and there leave it by bearing right onto a signposted bridleway that runs between walls. This walled track leads on to a gate giving into the bottom corner of a sloping pasture. Turn right alongside a fence, and keep forward through a gate, still beside a fence, and continue to reach a gravel track. Turn right on this to a footbridge spanning the Swale. This was damaged by flood water a few years ago and only reinstated in December 2002, at a cost of £113,000; hopefully it will prove more robust than the 1920s original.

**F** Over the bridge turn right to a narrow gate and continue on a grassy track across an enclosed pasture to a low footbridge giving onto a narrow walled track to the right of a barn.

Continue up the track. At the top, turn right for Reeth, though a thoughtfully positioned bench encourages a moment of retrospective viewing. The track shortly becomes a surfaced lane. Continue to the first turning on the left. Go left here (Langhorne Drive) and walk up to the main road and there turn right to return to the village green. ●

# Semer Water

| | |
| --- | --- |
| **Start** | Bainbridge |
| **Distance** | 8 miles (13km) |
| **Height gain** | 985ft (300m) |
| **Approximate time** | 4 hours |
| **Parking** | Around village green in Bainbridge |
| **Refreshments** | Pubs and cafés in Bainbridge |
| **Ordnance Survey maps** | Landranger 98 (Wensleydale & Upper Wharfedale), Explorer OL30 (Yorkshire Dales – Northern & Central areas) |

*Semer Water, one of only two natural lakes in the Yorkshire Dales, is surrounded by moors and thinly populated farmland. The lake itself is of modest size, but its setting is perfect, possessing an air of mystery and quiet intrigue. Beginning in the village of Bainbridge, this agreeable walk wanders easily across hillsides above the River Bain to the spread of Semer Water, before heading onto the moors to join a Roman road for the final stage back to Bainbridge.*

Bainbridge is arguably the most attractive village in Wensleydale, and developed as a base for foresters. Until fairly recently, the custom of blowing a forest horn each evening – as a guide to travellers in the forest – was still carried on, but, like so many ancient customs, has fallen from grace. The origins of the tradition are rooted in Saxon times, when the dalesfolk blew a horn to warn of danger or to instigate a hue and cry against poachers. In Norman times, strangers entering what had become the royal hunting Forest of Wensleydale, wolf-infested and overrun with deer and wild boar, were obliged to blow a horn to show they came with peaceful intent. Around Semer Water, a horn was sounded whenever a wolf was spotted near the isolated 'setts' so that the animals could be herded to safety. When the last wolf was killed in Britain,

the horn was still a signal to the farmers to move their livestock to fresh pastures.

Begin from the village green in Bainbridge by heading out in the Leyburn direction. After a short uphill stroll, leave the road just by a lay-by turning onto a path on the right signposted to Semer Water. The path climbs and shortly runs alongside a wall before branching across hillside pastures on a footpath that leads ultimately to a wall with two, gated gap-stiles. Take the stile on the right and follow a green path over a slight rise before descending to a wall corner. Then follow a path running beside the wall. Cross more hill pastures and descend to a ladder-stile. Having crossed the stile, follow a green path beside the River Bain to reach Semer Water Bridge **A**.

Semer Water is a product of the last

*Bainbridge village green*

Ice Age, formed by morainic debris which effectively dammed the whole valley. The lake is today only a shadow of its former self, but the river provides an interesting geological snippet. Unlike conventional rivers, the River Bain is blocked in its upper reaches by glacial drift. This has the effect of increasing the gradient lower down. So, the river starts off with a gentle gradient, becoming more energetic as it passes through the dale, and cutting through rock before finally producing waterfalls on the outskirts of Bainbridge.

The geological explanation of how the valley, known as Raydale, was formed is rather prosaic. Legend provides a more intriguing account. Here, it is said, an angel came one day disguised as a beggar, seeking food and shelter, but was turned away by everyone in the village, until, at last, the angel came to a ramshackle hut set a distance from the rest. Here the stranger was invited in to share the meagre possessions of the man and his wife who lived there. The next morning, the angel, being in an uncharacteristically vengeful mood, turned towards the village below, and brought forth great torrents from the hillsides that flooded the village and drowned all its inhabitants, save for the man and his wife. Just along the road from Semer Water Bridge stands Low Blean, said to be the house of the hospitable couple.

Go over the bridge, as if heading to nearby Countersett, and in a few strides leave the road for a footpath on the left signposted to Marsett Lane. The path crosses a number of fields to meet the lane at a step-stile. Turn left and follow the lane for about 550 yds (500m) as far as a footpath on the right for Countersett and Crag Side Road.

Turn onto the footpath and follow it towards farm buildings, climbing to the right of a stream to a gated gap-stile. In the next pasture, climb obliquely right to another stile in the top right-hand corner of the pasture. Head diagonally right up-field towards a powerline pole near a dilapidated wall corner, and there bear right to a gap-stile and left to

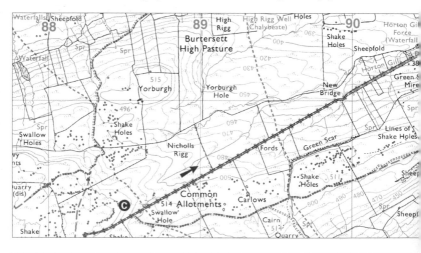

cross the corner of a hill pasture to climb to a ladder-stile above, giving onto Crag Side Road **B**.

Immediately leave the road through a gate on the left to pursue a broad track (signposted to Wether Fell). Follow the rising track to a gate and through this bear left to another gate, and then rising beyond on a green track.

The track leads up onto the moorland top and forward through two gates/ stiles, pressing on across the moor to intersect a footpath (signposted), near which another signpost points the way forward to the 'Roman road'. Keep on in the same direction to meet the broad, stony track of Cam High Road **C**, the Roman road between Ingleton and Bainbridge. At the road, turn right and walk in the footsteps of legionnaires all the way back to the outskirts of Bainbridge. At Four Lane Ends **D** cross the surfaced road linking Burtersett and Countersett. Beyond, Cam High Road sweeps on downhill across Bainbridge High Pasture to rejoin the Countersett road on the edge of Bainbridge. Now simply follow the surfaced road down into Bainbridge. ●

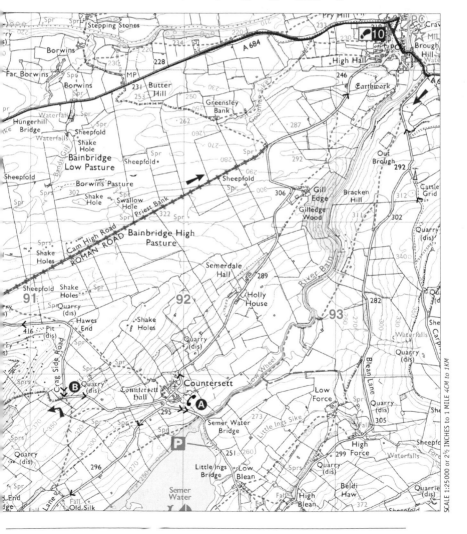

# Cam Head

| | |
|---|---|
| **Start** | Kettlewell |
| **Distance** | 6¼ miles (10km) |
| **Height gain** | 1065 ft (325m) |
| **Approximate time** | 3–4 hours |
| **Parking** | Kettlewell (Pay and Display) |
| **Refreshments** | Pubs and cafés in Kettlewell, pub at Starbotton |
| **Ordnance Survey maps** | Landranger 98 (Wensleydale & Upper Wharfedale), Explorer OL30 (Yorkshire Dales – Northern & Central areas) |

*A steady but fairly easy climb from Kettlewell to Cam Head along a walled green lane is followed by a winding descent along another green lane to the hamlet of Starbotton. The views over Wharfedale are extensive and superb, and the return to Kettlewell is an easy and agreeable walk down the Dales Way, which here uses meadows bordering the River Wharfe.*

Like many villages in the Yorkshire Dales, Kettlewell began as a small farming community, but later expanded as textile and then lead mining industries came into the area. Many of its houses and cottages belong to the heyday of those industries in the 18th and 19th centuries, including the Victorian church.

🖉 Begin by turning left out of the car park towards the village centre. Cross the bridge in front of the Bluebell

*Kettlewell from Top Mere Road*

Hotel and turn right, following the road to a junction near the post office. Keep ahead at this junction onto the Leyburn road, shortly turning left with it as it climbs a very steep gradient. A short way on, as the road bends to the right, leave it by going forward onto a walled, stony track **A**.

The track is Top Mere Road; it climbs steadily, though the gradient eases higher up, allowing time to take in the surrounding countryside.

Eventually, the enclosing wall ends, but the track maintains the same direction across the open moorland that rises to Cam Head where the people who lived in the valley came to gather peat for their fires. The track, now a wide and rutted affair, pushes on to meet another track, Starbotton Cam Road, at a signpost.

Go left here **B**, initially still climbing, then levelling before heading down to a gate giving into another

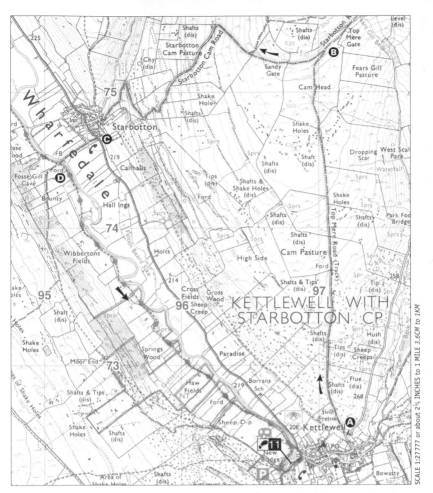

SCALE 1:27777 or about 2¼ INCHES to 1 MILE 3.6CM to 1KM

| 0 | 200 | 400 | 600 | 800 METRES | 1 |
|---|---|---|---|---|---|
| | | | | | KILOMETRES |
| | | | | | MILES |
| 0 | 200 | 400 | 600 YARDS | ½ | |

walled lane. This lane descends steadily, twisting and turning, as it leads down to Starbotton, providing lovely views up and down Wharfedale along the way.

On reaching the edge of Starbotton, turn left, walking through the streets to reach the valley road at the southern edge of the hamlet **C**. Cross the road with care into a signposted and walled path opposite that leads down to a bridge spanning the River Wharfe.

Like Kettlewell, Starbotton is also a legacy of the lead mining era, but is best remembered for its unusual name and the devastation it sustained in 1686 when Cam Gill Beck – that seemingly innocuous stream flowing down to the valley – became swollen during and

after a major storm, sending slurry and boulders down the hillside, causing damage to almost all the houses in the hamlet. It was by far the worst flooding ever experienced in the valley.

**D** Now turn left onto the Dales Way which takes the walk back to Kettlewell. The way generally parallels the river, with a few minor deviations, but provides a delightful and easy conclusion to the walk. Just on reaching Kettlewell, the path passes through a gate onto the riverbank and climbs briefly to the western edge of the road bridge, with the end of the walk only a few strides away. ●

# Burnsall and Linton

| | |
|---|---|
| **Start** | Burnsall |
| **Distance** | 6½ miles (10.3km) |
| **Approximate time** | 3 hours |
| **Parking** | Burnsall (charge) |
| **Refreshments** | Pubs and cafés in Burnsall, pub at Linton |
| **Ordnance Survey maps** | Landranger 98 (Wensleydale & Upper Wharfedale), Explorer OL2 (Yorkshire Dales – Southern & Western areas) |

*An agreeably relaxing walk through some of Wharfedale's finest scenery, embracing very pleasant riverside walking, an isolated church, two very attractive villages, and, if the river allows, some close encounters with stepping stones.*

Many visitors take the view that Burnsall is all that a Dales village should be with its meandering river, arched bridge, a village green, inn, church and Tudor grammar school. The scene is beautiful from every angle.

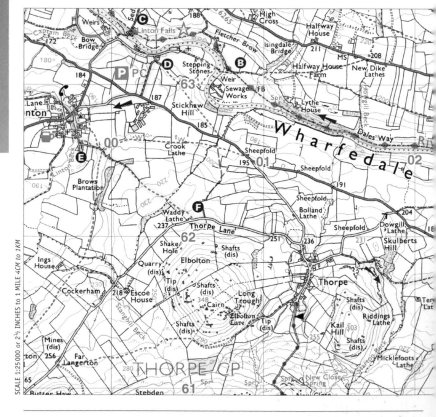

SCALE 1:25 000 or 2½ INCHES to 1 MILE 4CM to 1KM

Leave the village by crossing the end of its bridge onto a Dales Way footpath that turns immediately right, near the Red Lion pub, to gain the riverbank. A constructed path now leads past the ancient grammar school, founded in 1602, and Burnsall church, which dates from the 14th century.

The path hugs the riverbank all the while, passing shortly through the gorge of Loup Scar. Continue easily to a suspension bridge **A**, by which the river is crossed. The bridge was built by public subscription in the 19th century to replace the stepping stones downriver, though, if the water is very low and your sense of balance good, the stepping stones can still be used – but, please, no heroics here.

On the other side of the bridge, turn immediately left and continue along the true left bank of the Wharfe down an avenue of chestnut, beech and oak trees. Continue following the riverside path, but gradually as the low profile of Linton church comes into view, so the path moves temporarily away from the river, to a gate giving onto a broad

track **B**. Just before the gate, another line of stepping stones crosses the river, leading directly to Linton church, but, other than to investigate them, these should be ignored.

Continue along the stony track, which later becomes a surfaced lane. Leave it as it bends right, passing through a gated gap on the left onto a signposted footpath for Grassington and Linton Falls. Now strike across a field, moving back towards the river, across which lies the squat Church of St Michael's and All Angels. Keep heading upriver towards a bridge spanning the river at Linton Falls **C**. This is the fourth bridge to occupy this site; the first, known as Tin Bridge, was built in 1814 and was covered with sheets of metal from old oil drums, hence the name. The present bridge was built in 1989.

Across the bridge turn right along an enclosed walkway that leads to Little Emily's Bridge, an attractive packhorse bridge on the original church path from Threshfield. It is thought to have been named after a member of the Norton family who took refuge nearby at the time of the Civil War.

Turn away from Little Emily's Bridge and go up steps to a road. Turn left, and head for Linton church. Just before the last house on the right, about 55 yds (50m) past a small parking area, look for a track leading off to the right. *Anyone wanting to visit Linton church should simply continue ahead and then return to this turning.*

**D** Turn onto the track, and at the back of the house, where the path forks, bear right onto an enclosed path that climbs alongside a wall at a field edge, and runs on to meet a lane. Turn right; the road almost immediately forks. Branch left, following the side road towards the village of Linton. At the edge of Linton, keep left to reach Linton

Beck. Just before the beck bridge, turn left again, and walk initially alongside the stream – the village green and pub are on the other side.

Follow a surfaced lane to its far end, and there turn left onto a footpath for Thorpe Lane **E**. Pass around a farmyard to gain a rough track between walls, and then starts to climb gently along the edge of hill pasture. The track accompanies the wall across a few fields, and then reaches a ladder-stile beside a gate. From the stile, follow a grassy path across a sloping pasture, the route being waymarked by boulders, yellow-topped poles and signposts, and eventually meeting Thorpe Lane.

**F** Turn left along Thorpe Lane, a lovely single track road, walled on both sides and with a rich green strip down its centre. At a road junction, bear right towards Thorpe, and when the road forks near the village centre, bear left.

Thorpe lies hidden among reef knolls, a characteristic that more than likely saved it from the attention of marauding Scots in years gone by. Also known as Thorpe-in-the-Hollow, the village is mainly a gathering of houses, cottages, a manor house and busy farms. When Fountains Abbey flourished, Thorpe had a reputation for producing shoes and slippers for the monks.

Go past the Manor House, after which the road climbs a little. As it bends to the left, leave it by branching right onto a track, signposted for Burnsall. The path sets off between walls, and descends to a gated gap-stile on the right. Through this, continue down the ongoing track to a gate. Beyond, the path remains clear, and crosses a succession of undulating and enclosed pastures, pressing on to intercept and cross a rough track (Badger Lane) **G**. It then continues much as before, across undulating fields, but now with Burnsall in view ahead. Gradually, the height is lost, and the path runs on as a grassy strip across numerous fields, eventually reaching Burnsall.

Turn right and follow the road round to the Red Lion pub, and back to the start of the walk. ●

*Little Emily's Bridge, Linton*

# Aysgarth Falls and Bolton Castle

| | |
|---|---|
| **Start** | Aysgarth Falls |
| **Distance** | 6 miles (10km) |
| **Approximate time** | 3–4 hours |
| **Parking** | Visitor centre car park at Aysgarth Falls |
| **Refreshments** | Café at Aysgarth Falls, restaurant at Castle Bolton and pub in Carperby |
| **Ordnance Survey maps** | Landranger 98 (Wensleydale & Upper Wharfedale), Explorer OL30 (Yorkshire Dales – Northern & Central areas) |

*A pleasure at any time of year, but especially beautiful in spring, this delightful circuit from Aysgarth to the village of Castle Bolton and back is easy walking. Lord Scrope's great endeavour, the ancient Bolton Castle, considered to be 'a climax of English military architecture', is an added pleasure.*

Set off from the National Park visitor centre at Aysgarth and walk out to the road, following a fenced pathway to the right, shortly crossing the road and going through a gate on a path (signposted to Middle Falls and Lower Falls). The path leads into Freeholder's Wood, which is an ancient woodland where the National Park authority have reintroduced traditional coppicing to regenerate the wood and provide wildlife habitats. Some of the residents of nearby Carperby still have rights of estover in Freeholder's Wood, i.e. the right to take wood, usually for burning, house or hedge repairs, from a forest.

*A brief diversion, right, down steps visits the Middle Falls, a splendid sight when the river is in spate*; return to the main path and turn right, and press on to the Lower Falls. Another short deviation leads to these falls. On the way out, at a path junction, turn right and follow the ongoing path above the river to a stile. Over this, go forward beside an intermittent hedgerow on the left to a fence. Here turn right and walk beside the fence to a stile.

Cross the ensuing field in much the same direction, but bearing slightly left towards Hollin House Farm. Go through the farmyard, and on reaching open pastureland keep forward a short distance before leaving the access, at a signpost, for a track bearing right to a stile in a distant wall.

In the pasture beyond, go forward on a green track with Bolton Castle now in view ahead. The track leads down to a wall and fence junction. Here cross a stile over a fence (do not go through the gap-stile in the adjoining wall), and turn right on a rutted track, and follow the wall. Go over a step-stile and a gap-stile a few strides later, and then continue with the wall on your right. When the wall bends right, leave it and go forward on another green path that moves across to accompany a wall forward to enter the enclosed Thoresby Lane **A**.

Follow the lane to Low Thoresby Farm, where the track becomes surfaced. Go around the farm and out to meet the road on the edge of Redmire. Turn left.

About 65 yds (60m) after the road bends to the left, leave it, on the right, through a gap-stile **B**, and then follow an obvious green path across a series of fields linked by stiles. At one stage the path crosses the trackbed of the former Wensleydale Railway, before continuing into Castle Bolton. At the village, turn left and walk towards the castle.

The castle was built in 1379 for Richard de Scrope, Lord Chancellor of England between 1378 and 1380, at the start of Richard II's reign. Lord Scrope (1327-1403), a retainer of John of Gaunt, Duke of Lancaster, raised his family to the peerage by a career of unremitting service on the battlefield and in administration, which included being Warden of the West March in the troubled regions of the Anglo-Scottish border. He was the eldest surviving son of Chief Justice Henry Scrope, and was

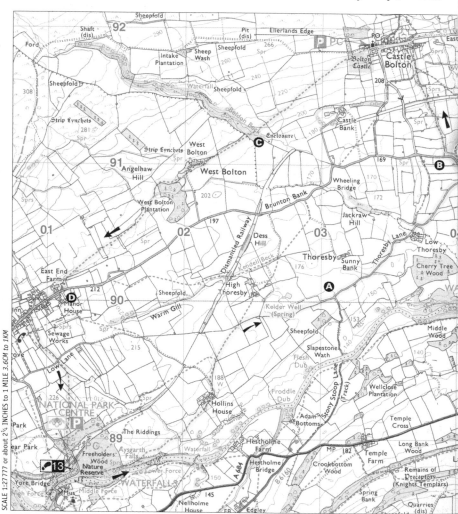

*Bolton Castle*

occasionally denigrated for his lowly origins. Today, his massive fortress is one of the best preserved in the country, and dominates the surrounding countryside it was built to defend.

Go past the church of St Oswald, with the castle on the left, and along a broad track to pass a car park. Just after a gate across the track, leave it, and bear left to a gap-stile in a field corner. Cross a small enclosure, and then from a wall corner descend obliquely across a wide, open pasture on a footpath signposted to Aysgarth.

On the far side, pass through the left-hand one of two metal gates, and on across another pasture. In the third field, descend to cross Beldon Beck by a footbridge **C**, rising beyond to another stile. Then continue across fields to West Bolton Farm. Go directly in front of the farm buildings on its access track to locate a gated gap-stile on the right. The ongoing path passes to the north of a small plantation, and then goes on to cross a stream. Over the stream bear right to a stile, and then keep on along an obvious green track across a number of pastures.

The track eventually goes down to pass another farm and meet the main road **D** on the edge of Carperby. Turn right along the road into the village as far as the Wheatsheaf pub and turn left onto a footpath directly opposite (signposted to Aysgarth). Cross a stream to enter an elongated pasture, and go forward with a wall on the right. Pass a metal gate and then leave the pasture at a gap-stile, on the right, about 165 yds (150m) from the road. Through the stile, turn left, and walk beside a wall to reach Low Lane. Cross the lane and go through a gap-stile, and then keep forward with a wall on the right.

When the wall ends go through another stile, and then left across a number of fields on an obvious grassy path. A final gate and gap-stile leads into the top edge of Freeholder's Wood. Follow a path through the wood, initially right and then descending left to a gate giving onto the road. Turn left and go beneath an old railway bridge, and immediately turn right to return to the visitor centre car park.  ●

*Burnsall, Trollers Gill and Appletreewick*

# Burnsall, Trollers Gill and Appletreewick

| | |
|---|---|
| **Start** | Burnsall |
| **Distance** | 7 miles (11km) |
| **Approximate time** | 3½ hours |
| **Parking** | Burnsall (charge) |
| **Refreshments** | Pubs and cafés in Burnsall, pubs in Appletreewick |
| **Ordnance Survey maps** | Landrangers 98 (Wensleydale & Upper Wharfedale), 99 (Northallerton & Ripon) and 104 (Leeds & Bradford), Explorer OL2 (Yorkshire Dales – Southern & Western areas) |

*Two villages, breezy and open moorland, a spectacular ravine and lush riverside meadows combine to make this an agreeably varied walk over countryside that lies between Wharfedale and the more easterly Nidderdale. The ascent, though long, is gradual, and the road walking is along generally quiet roads.*

There are two main parking areas in Burnsall: a small car park at the edge of the village, and a large riverside meadow just east of Burnsall Bridge; free parking in the village is limited and usually snapped up early in the day.

🥾 Cross Burnsall Bridge and set off along the road for Appletreewick, and, *taking care against approaching traffic,* follow this through the hamlet of Hartlington. Continue to cross the sizeable Barben Beck and on for another 220 yds (200m), leaving the road at a stile and gate **A** on the left giving onto a bridleway for 'New Road'. This starts as a stony track through a shallow ravine, soon emerging to climb beside a wall.

The route, with fine views over Wharfedale, is well signposted and/or shepherded along enclosed tracks, leading first to a group of farm buildings. Here, turn through a gate and keep on along another walled track (still

signposted for New Road). When the walls end at a gate, continue to follow the broad track which now crosses upland pasture. Eventually, the track sweeps on across moorland to reach New Road at a gate **B**. *For the ½ mile*

(800m) the track is decidedly more evident than the bridleway shown on the map which, largely indistinguishable on the ground, veers first to the right of the track and then to the left, meeting New Road at a corner. A signpost at the road gate suggests that use of the track is acceptable.

Turn left to follow the road, and about 80 yds (70m) after the road bends sharply to the right, leave it at a footpath on the right for Skyreholme, following a waymarked route across rough pasture to intercept a field vehicle track. A short way on the vehicle track sweeps down and to the right following a right of way down to Skyreholme Beck. However, a permissive path (waymarked) branches left from this, where the track turns to the right **C**. Take to the permissive path, and follow this to meet the upper section of Skyreholme Beck **D**, and there, still following the permissive

path, turn right, descending with care into the rocky ravine of Trollers Gill.

Trollers Gill is a miniature gorge through the Great Scar limestone, narrow, dark and steep-sided and the classic lair of monsters; indeed, one such resides here, the Barguest, the spectral hound of Craven, a huge, shaggy beast, with yellow eyes as big as saucers. An encounter with the Barguest means almost certain death, few have escaped to tell of it, though there are a number of records of close encounters with the beast.

At the bottom of the gill, the Trollers Gill route and that which followed the vehicle track combine at a step-stile. Over the stile, keep forward on a terraced path above Skyreholme Beck and pass a large grass-covered mound that once formed the dam of a reservoir that served the Skyreholme paper mills. Eventually, the descending track meets a road near the entrance to Parceval

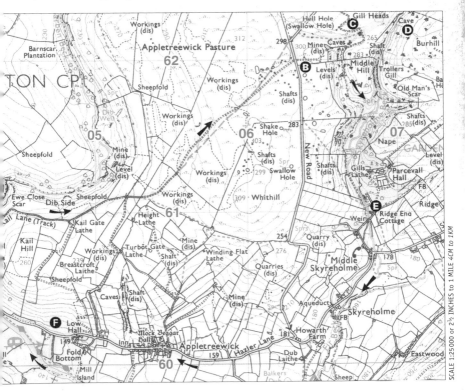

*Looking towards Trollers Gill*

Hall and Grounds **E**. The hall was built in 1671, but has an Elizabethan look about it. It is generally regarded as the finest residential building in Wharfedale; the surrounding gardens and tearoom are open to the public from Easter until the end of October.

Turn right along the road and continue down to a road junction, there turning right, passing a telephone box, and beginning a long stretch of road walking (*take care against traffic*). The road rolls on through Middle Skyreholme and Skyreholme and eventually reaches a road junction. Turn left and continue to Appletreewick.

Appletreewick has more than its share of claims to fame. Of Norse origin, it is recorded in the *Domesday Book* as in the ownership of the English thanes (low-ranking nobles), Dolfin and Orme. This is a one street village, but few are better than this. Fine old buildings line the street from High Hall to Low Hall, and passing by far the best, Mock Beggar Hall, which housed the monks in charge of Bolton Priory's lands

hereabouts. But the village is also renowned for a real-life Dick Whittington character, William Craven, born here in 1548. He was sent to London to be apprentice to a merchant tailor and grew in stature and standing to become Sheriff and later Lord Mayor of London.

Press on down through the village, finally leaving the road at the edge of a caravan site by turning left onto a walled footpath **F** for the riverside. On reaching the river, turn right, now following the Dales Way riverside path.

The path leads on to pass Woodhouse Farm **G**, a 17th-century manor house, and once the home of the almost forgotten Wharfedale poet, John Atkinson Bland. Beyond the farm, a footbridge takes the route over Barben Beck once more. From the beck, continue across another field to a gate, after which the path runs on above the Wharfe and finally crosses a large field, used as a car park during summer months, to reach the road. Turn left to recross Burnsall Bridge and return to the start of the walk. ●

# Ribblehead and Chapel le Dale

| | |
|---|---|
| **Start** | Ribblehead |
| **Distance** | 6¾ miles (10.8km) |
| **Approximate time** | 3½ hours |
| **Parking** | Near Station Inn, Ribblehead |
| **Refreshments** | Pubs at Ribblehead and Chapel le Dale |
| **Ordnance Survey maps** | Landranger 98 (Wensleydale & Upper Wharfedale), Explorer OL2 (Yorkshire Dales – Southern & Western areas) |

*Few can fail to be impressed by the engineering work that between 1869 and 1875 built the Ribblehead viaduct as part of the development of a new route to Scotland from London. It dominates the beginning and end of this walk, though much less so than the bulky fells on either side that culminate to the north in Whernside and to the south in Ingleborough. Most of the walk is flat and easy going, allowing time to contemplate the pastoral surroundings. Some amusement may be found in the abrupt disappearance and re-appearance of streams, a blessing in disguise as crossing them in spate would almost certainly produce wet feet.*

Set off along the broad track just to the east of the Station Inn, which heads directly for Whernside and the viaduct. As it nears the latter, so it swings left to pass beneath it, and then continues uneventfully towards Gunnerfleet Farm.

The viaduct is a stark reminder of the Midland Railway's determination to construct its own route to Scotland. It was built at enormous cost both in terms of finance and of human life. In the 1980s, affected by the ravages of time and the sheer inhospitability of the climate, the future of the Settle–Carlisle line was called very much into question as the old spectre of financial viability reared its head. During this time a

vigorous campaign was waged to keep the line open, and all the effort that went into the campaign was at last vindicated in April 1989, when the Government announced that the line was to remain open. It will long remain as a testament to Victorian endeavour and achievement. From 1989 into the early 1990s, the viaduct saw massive repair work, funded by a consortium comprising British Rail (as it then was), English Heritage, local authorities and other interested bodies, and designed to resolve a problem of water seepage and falling masonry.

After Gunnerfleet Farm, cross Winterscales Beck and turn left along a surfaced field track **Ⓐ**. Shortly after

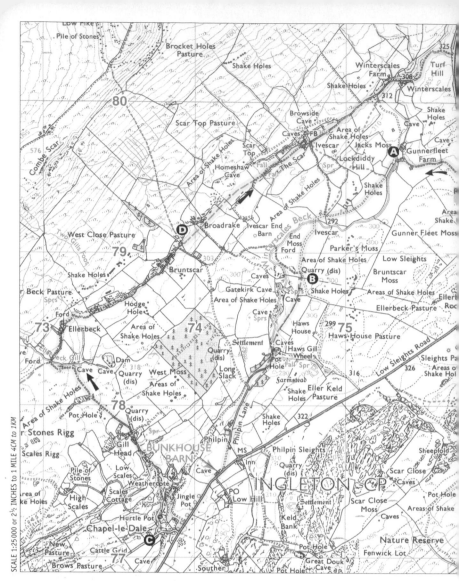

passing through a metal gate, the lane re-crosses Winterscales Beck. Continue as far as another gate beside a cattle-grid **B**, and beyond this, leave the lane by branching right onto a grassy track leading to a gate in a wall corner. Keep forward alongside a wall and fence. As the wall bends sharply left, keep ahead, descending towards Winterscales Beck, which, at the crossing point, usually contrives to disappear conveniently underground for a short distance: *in spate conditions, retreat.*

Otherwise, cross to a gate in a corner,

and walk on to another a few strides away, and then go forward along the bottom edge of a sloping pasture with a line of larch trees on the right. Bear slightly left to a narrow gate giving into a rocky gully, often flooded (*but by-passable in the adjacent field if the right of way is effectively obstructed*). The gully has limestone as its bedrock, which is slippery when wet. It leads out to join a surfaced lane (Philpin Lane), which is followed out past Philpin Farm to meet the B6255.

Turn right and, *taking care against*

| 0 | 200 | 400 | 600 | 800 METRES | 1 |
| 0 | 200 | 400 | 600 YARDS | ½ | KILOMETRES MILES |

*approaching traffic*, follow the road for 550 yds (500m), as far as the turning on the right to Chapel le Dale church. Leave the main road here, and walk up to the church.

**C** Immediately after the church, take the lane on the right, and follow this, ascending steadily to a cattle-grid just beyond which lies Hurtle Pot, a deep hole, its walls swathed in ferns and mosses.

When the ongoing track forks, keep forward (signposted for Ellerbeck) and now on a rough track climbing through an area of mossy boulders and trees. Keep following the track towards Ellerbeck, and, just before the farm, turn right at a shallow ford, and continue up to the farm. There follows an obvious route between the buildings to reach the start of a broad track that takes a gently descending course across sloping pastures.

Keep forward along an obvious track, passing a

few farmsteads and eventually reaching a track junction where the route divides with one branch (left) going up beside a barn towards Whernside. At this point **D**, keep forward (to the right of the barn), through a narrow gate onto a bridleway (signposted for Winterscales). From the gate the route continues as a broad grassy track that crosses a pasture and soon leads to another farm. Go past this, and just after the farm the ongoing route once more becomes a grassy track across the top edge of a pasture.

After two more narrow gates, the route passes into a more open area, crossing eventually to a gate and signpost beyond at a stream crossing. A short way ahead, the track reaches a house and more farms. At the complex of farm buildings at Ivescar, maintain the same direction, following a surfaced lane.

At a track junction near Winterscales Farm, keep ahead over a stile and cattle-grid (signposted to Deepdale), and go past the farm, keeping to the right of the infant Winterscales Beck and soon pass the last of the farm buildings and onto a rising track that curves round to a tunnel beneath the railway at Bleamoor Sidings. Through the tunnel turn right along a constructed path that leads on to rejoin the outward route near the Ribblehead viaduct. ●

*Ribblehead viaduct*

# Kettlewell and Arncliffe

| | |
|---|---|
| **Start** | Kettlewell |
| **Distance** | 6 miles (9.8km) |
| **Height gain** | 1510ft (460m) |
| **Approximate time** | 4 hours |
| **Parking** | Kettlewell (Pay and Display) |
| **Refreshments** | Pubs and cafés in Kettlewell, pub and café at Arncliffe |
| **Ordnance Survey maps** | Landranger 98 (Wensleydale & Upper Wharfedale), Explorer OL30 (Yorkshire Dales – Northern & Central areas) |

*Two dales are included in this walk, which starts from Kettlewell in Wharfedale and climbs steeply across rugged moorland to drop down into Littondale. A delightful stretch alongside the River Skirfare follows before another up-and-over section, rather less demanding than the earlier one, crosses the shoulder of the hills for a stunning view over Wharfedale.*

Kettlewell lies on the banks of the Wharfe, surrounded by steep hillsides and moorlands criss-crossed by drystone walls. From the car park the route begins by crossing the Wharfe bridge and immediately turning right, but taking the left-hand one of two tracks, one that rises to a gate and a signpost for Arncliffe. Almost immediately, leave the stony track by branching left onto an ascending path that soon climbs to a through-stile beyond which the path rises more steeply to a limestone scar above.

Pass through the scar by a narrow, rocky gully and continue climbing beyond onto moorland, following a grassy path to a signpost at a cross-track, from which it maintains the same direction, still climbing to reach a ladder-stile over a wall. Over this bear left, parallel with the wall, still climbing but now at an easier gradient. Gradually the route moves away from the wall, bearing right across a low limestone plateau but later climbing through a low limestone lip, above which the path heads for another ladder-stile.

After the stile, continue across the top of the ridge to another stile **Ⓐ**, where the descent to Arncliffe begins as a grassy track across heather moorland. Continue descending to a footpath sign where the track bears right, continuing steadily downwards to a ladder-stile spanning an intake wall at the top edge of mixed woodland. Drop down through the woodland.

The descending path eventually reaches the valley road **B**. Cross to a narrow gate opposite and walk beside the River Skirfare passing the church. On the far side of the field, go left over the river bridge and walk round to the church.

*Here, the route has only touched on the lovely village of Arncliffe, and it is worth taking a short break from the route to explore a little farther.*

Go past the lychgate and onto a path beside the churchyard (signposted for Hawkswick), leading through to a riverside pasture. The riverside path is never in doubt, continuing downstream as a mainly grassy track at varying distances from the river, but finally being channelled in towards a footbridge **C** spanning the river and giving onto a narrow lane beyond. Turn right and walk into Hawkswick.

Leave the village road at a footpath on the left, signposted for Kettlewell, and turning up a stony track between cottages. After a stile the track forks. Branch left and soon curve round above the intake wall. As it gains height the path moves away from the wall, and continues to climb across the shoulder of Hawkswick Moor. The path climbs steadily to a large cairn **D** and there bears left, still climbing to gain the ridge at a ladder-stile.

Over the stile take the higher of two paths (they soon rejoin), and begin an outstanding high level trek northwards, for the most part descending gently and finally crossing a couple of ladder-stiles to enter a small plantation. Follow the path down and around the edge of the plantation to reach a ruined building. Pass in front of this (i.e. to the right), and continue descending across a lightly wooded slope to emerge onto the valley road. Turn left to return to Kettlewell and the start of the walk.  ●

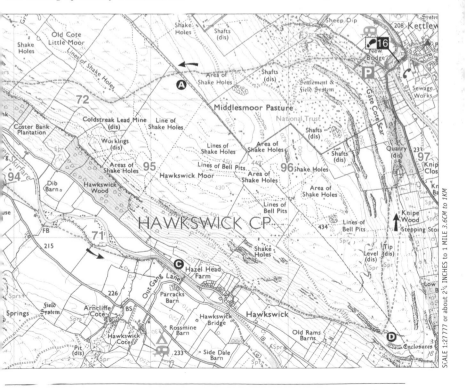

*Around Malham*

# Around Malham

| | |
|---|---|
| **Start** | Malham |
| **Distance** | 7 miles (11km) |
| **Height gain** | 640ft (195m) |
| **Approximate time** | 3–4 hours |
| **Parking** | Malham (Pay and Display) |
| **Refreshments** | Pubs and cafés in Malham |
| **Ordnance Survey maps** | Landranger 98 (Wensleydale & Upper Wharfedale), Explorer OL2 (Yorkshire Dales – Southern and Western areas) |

*An easy walk through spectacular limestone scenery. A little scrambling is called for in Gordale, made intimidating by the cascading falls, but not as difficult as it looks. Above the falls a wide limestone plateau opens up to Malham Tarn, followed by a delightful amble back to the top of Malham Cove – but the true splendour of this walk derives from its wealth of geological and botanical interest.*

The origins of Malham go back to AD700, to a simple settlement centred on the present village green. Around AD1100, the village was cut in two when the beck became the boundary of lands owned by Fountains Abbey and Bolton Priory. Henry VIII's Dissolution of the Monasteries, however, brought new prosperity, replacing old wooden houses by stone buildings that still form the core of the village today. Also surviving to present times is the humped packhorse bridge, built across the beck in 1636.

📝 Leave the car park and follow the road for a short distance towards the village centre. Keep an eye open for a small footbridge across the beck on the right, and use it to gain and follow downstream a broad path on the opposite side (signposted 'Janet's Foss'). A stile gives access to a meadow, the path keeping to its edge, beside the stream. Shortly, pass through a gate not far from an old stone barn, and here change direction. The onward route passing the barn is never in doubt, and leads to a small woodland flanking Gordale Beck, in spring permeated by the strong and garlicky smell of wild ramsons which flower from April to June and especially like damp woodlands.

The head of this shallow gorge is taken by a waterfall, Janet's Foss Ⓐ. Here, white water tumbles over a lip of tufa into a crystal plunge pool. Tufa is similar to stalagmite in that it, too, is calcium carbonate precipitated from lime-saturated water. Unlike stalagmite, tufa is formed in a surface stream where algae grow and cause the precipitation by altering the chemistry of the water. Along Gordale Beck there are many spots where you will find tufa, some inactive, but some, as at Janet's Foss, still forming. It is most evident at the Foss in the way it projects over a rock ledge to create the cave behind the falls where a legendary fairy queen, Janet, once lived.

Near the falls a narrow gully leads to a path and a metalled road. Turn right along the road and follow it for a short distance, the towering cliffs of Gordale Scar now in evidence ahead. At a gate on the left, enter beckside pastureland (often used as a camp site) and you can take a path into the very jaws of the chasm. Arguments still rumble quietly as to how this unique rock architecture came into being, some propounding the view that it once formed an enormous cavern which in later times collapsed, leaving only its walls standing, but there is little real doubt that it was cut by retreating meltwater flowing from Ice Age glaciers.

The path into the gorge gives no indication of what awaits around a sharp corner, for here the walls close in dramatically, 165ft (50m) high and barely 50ft (15m) separating them at one point, severely overhanging at their base, and vertical at their easiest angle. Higher still, more crags and scars continue upwards to the plateau surface above the beck. Hidden from external view, a fine waterfall gushes through an eyehole in a thin wall of limestone, pauses in its downward flight in a natural amphitheatre, and spills splendidly to the broad base of the chasm floor. Close by the eyehole falls, which are actively depositing tufa on a bank below, a larger bank of inactive tufa, to the left, marks the site of an earlier waterfall. This was active until 250–300 years ago when the beck suddenly discovered its new route through the eyehole.

Many walkers elect to retreat from this point to find an alternative route to Malham Tarn (*see final paragraph*), but by splashing through the shallows it is easy enough (in all but spate conditions) to reach the base of a prominent buttress of banded and inactive tufa dividing the falls, which, improbable though it may seem, offers an entertaining scramble to the sanctuary of the upper gorge. You will get wet, so a small towel and spare socks will help. As with most seemingly difficult things, the start of the scramble poses the problem, but once actually on the rock, the way up is easy – something I've done variously with my father (in his 70s), mother-in-law (in her 60s), young children, and two dogs. If you do not feel confident about it, then opt for the variant route.

A good path climbs easily away from the gorge which, from above, can clearly be recognised as a meltwater channel with rocky walls, and across a wide plateau of limestone, the limestone pavement for which this region is so renowned. The path, absorbed now by a rich green fescue turf, broadens and presses on to reach another metalled road (*it would lead, left, back to Malham should the need arise*).

However it is the limestone pavement to which the botanist will be attracted, for the range of plant life is immense,

---

*Janet's Foss, Malham*

and quite remarkable. The fissures between the blocks (clints) of limestone are called grykes, and in them, protected from sun and the attentions of sheep, a rich variety of woodland and cliff-face species of plant exists. Hart's Tongue Fern is but one of a dozen ferns growing side by side with herb robert, wood sorrel, dog's mercury and, in a few secluded spots, baneberry. The turfed areas, too, have a wealth of flora: violets, fairy flax, bedstraws and birdsfoot-trefoil.

Follow the road for a short distance and continue to a minor crossroad. Just before the junction the route crosses the North Craven Fault, which marks the end of limestone pavements, for the rock ahead, supporting Malham Tarn, is impermeable slate. Keep ahead, and follow a graded track towards Lings Plantation **B**, where a left turn, leaving the main track, shortly leads to the outflow of the tarn, a natural lake. A small dam, built in 1791, stabilises the level of the lake, the overflow of which, Malham Water, flows south under the road and across the North Craven Fault where it encounters limestone and promptly disappears underground at a spot labelled, unimaginatively, Water Sinks.

The scenery around Malham and its tarn has been the inspiration of many, including John Ruskin, and Charles Kingsley, who wrote part of *The Water-Babies* while at Malham Tarn House as a guest of millionaire Walter Morrison. Charles Darwin, too, found the unrivalled setting conducive to his studies.

By following the line of the stream issuing from Malham Tarn the route regains the road. Turn right to cross the stream and reach a gate and a path on the opposite bank **C**.

Logic suggests that the waters from Malham Tarn are those which emerge in

due course at the foot of Malham Cove, but this is not so. Tests were first carried out in the 1870s, and again 100 years later, which demonstrate that the waters of Malham Tarn issue at Aire Head Springs, to the south of Malham village. For this reason Malham became famous

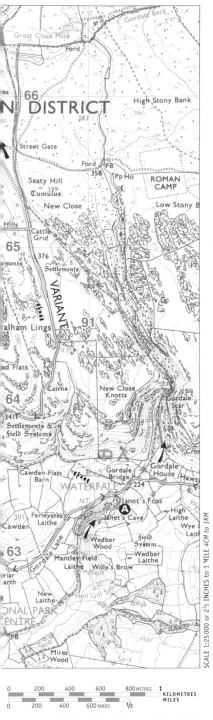

| 0 | 200 | 400 | 600 | 800 METRES | 1 |
| | | | | | KILOMETRES |
| | | | | | MILES |
| 0 | 200 | 400 | 600 YARDS | ½ | |

limestone hydrology.

The water from Malham Tarn disappears sullenly into stream bed debris, and from the spot, follow a path into a deepening dry valley, though the limestone underfoot can be slippery, until it curves sharply to avoid a dry waterfall, Comb Scar. Here the path doubles about to gain a stile at the head of a tributary gully which gives easy access to the floor of Watlowes, which about 14,000 years ago carried a powerful meltwater river. In those distant times the limestone was still frozen, of course, and prevented the water sinking underground as it does today.

Ahead now lies the lip of Malham Cove, and this unsuspecting approach is infinitely more dramatic and awe-inspiring than the easy walk from the village. No one can fail to be impressed by the landscape, which is nothing short of spectacular, and justifies its popularity on that score. The last few strides to the lip of the cove are over slippery limestone pavement, with only distant views to suggest there might be an abrupt drop ahead. Walkers with a good head for heights can approach the very edge for an aerial perspective of the people below: *anyone else should stay well clear.*

Across to the right, the limestone pavement may easily be followed to a couple of stiles at the top of a staircase. Only a few minutes are needed to descend to the valley floor, where a left turn will lead to the base of the cliff. In the centre, where a small dry valley cuts in, the height of the wall is 230ft (70m). The span of the cove is about 655ft (200m), with grassy ledges reaching in from the edges, but never quite meeting in the middle. Malham Beck, the infant River Aire, here issues from a small pool at the foot of the cliff, and despite cave-diving efforts, limited by a low

as one of the places where it was shown that underground streams are capable of crossing over one another independently in a complex system of underground passage, the caves behind the cove remain a mystery.

After leaving the cliffs of Malham Cove, watch for a clapper bridge on the left  crossing the stream to a gate. From the gate climb diagonally right to a small plateau of fescue turf and continue ascending gently to a prominent stile beyond which a good path works its way back to Malham by a succession of narrow walled lanes, reaching the village close by the humped packhorse bridge and the village green.

Leaving the cove is like passing through an open museum of farming history. The drystone walls across the valley date from the Enclosure Acts, about 200 years ago. Above the beck may be observed a series of horizontal ledges, linchets, or lynchets, built almost 1,000 years ago to improve the land, while low grass ridges across the valley floor, better picked out in late evening sunlight from above the cove, are now all that remain of Celtic field boundaries from about 2,000 years ago.

*Walkers not wishing to tackle the ascent of Gordale Scar, should simply retreat to the road and walk back towards Janet's Foss, but only as far as a bridge on the right. Here, go through a gate onto a path signposted for Malham Cove. Cross the ensuing field to a wall corner and then bear right, uphill, beside a wall. Cross a ladder-stile and another field to go up steps to a gate. Bear left along a clear path beside a wall. Beyond another gate, the path continues climbing steadily, curving right to a kissing-gate giving onto a lane. Turn right and follow the lane, and in due course, rejoin the original line.*

*The Dry Valley, Malham*

# Buckden and Langstrothdale Chase

| | |
|---|---|
| **Start** | Buckden |
| **Distance** | 7 miles (11km) |
| **Approximate time** | 3½ hours |
| **Parking** | Buckden |
| **Refreshments** | Pub and café in Buckden, pub at Cray, pub at Hubberholme |
| **Ordnance Survey maps** | Landranger 98 (Wensleydale & Upper Wharfedale), Explorer OL30 (Yorkshire Dales – Northern & Central areas) |

*This walk climbs to the tiny hamlet of Cray from Buckden, before heading across the southern slopes of Yockenthwaite Moor to Scar House, where the Quaker tradition flourished strongly in the 17th and 18th centuries. From there the high level traverse continues until the route drops to Yockenthwaite to begin a return leg along a delightful riverside section of the Dales Way.*

Buckden, which means the 'valley of the bucks', has been the abode of deer since medieval times, part of an ancient hunting forest. It is a beautiful place, hemmed in on all sides by rounded fellsides and wild moorland.

🖊 Go through a gate at the northern end of the car park, and head up a wide track that ascends easily through Rakes Wood. At first the track rises through trees and rocks, but higher up becomes more open; as a gate is approached so the angle of ascent eases, and soon a track deviates uphill towards higher ground. Ignore this, it leads up to Buckden Pike. Instead, continue ahead along the level edge of a limestone escarpment.

At a wall and gate with a narrow stile to the right, squeeze through the stile and keep ahead for a short distance to a narrow gate, where a footpath sign indicates a descent to Cray way below. The elevation gained thus far provides a splendid view of the limestone scenery of Upper Wharfedale and Langstrothdale.

From the gate the descent to Cray is

*Buckden Pike and Langstrothdale*

steep at first and leads down beside a wall to a footpath sign, and on to a gate. Cray Gill is crossed by a shallow ford, to meet the road. Continue behind the White Lion pub **Ⓐ** onto a broad farm track for Yockenthwaite. Two tracks are encountered, with the higher proving to be the better route, leading to a gate where the onward route to Scar House is signposted. From the gate the continuation is clear enough, and follows the edge of the escarpment, with only one slight deviation to cross Crook Gill by a footbridge. Keep ahead along a level grassy ledge.

The ongoing path closes in on a wall, and squeezes round its edge directly above Hubberholme, before continuing less evenly and trending right to keep above the intake wall, soon to reach Scar House **Ⓑ**, once a lively place of worship.

Scar House is a place where the new religion of the Quakers flourished. The Society of Friends, as it became known, was largely inspired by George Fox, whose vision on Pendle Hill of 'a great

*Buckden and Buckden Pike*

people in white raiment by a riverside, coming to the Lord' sent him preaching across the northern parts of England. George Fox is known to have visited Scar House twice, in 1652 and 1677, though it is unlikely the remains of Scar House that appear today are of the actual house he knew.

The ongoing route continues easily enough above Langstrothdale, a hunting forest that was the preserve of

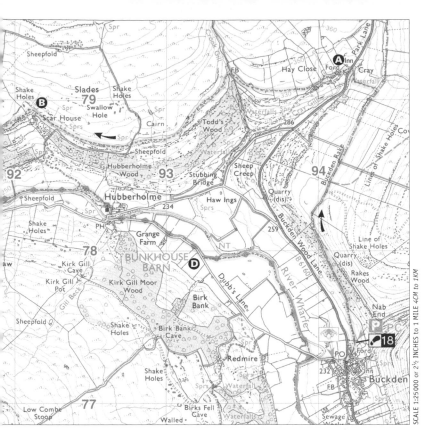

SCALE 1:25 000 or 2½ INCHES to 1 MILE 4CM to 1KM

the earls of Northumberland. The valley was originally settled by Norse farmers, and their legacy remains in the place names – Hubberholme and Yockenthwaite – which are still in use.

Pass round the back of Scar House and continue across limestone pavement to a gate and gap-stile in a wall. The looping path, less obvious now, continues along the southern edges of Yockenthwaite Moor before descending to the hamlet of the same name **C**, where the Dales Way is encountered.

Near the river, turn left along a track at a footpath sign for Hubberholme. Follow the track through a gate and cross a small field to a stile. Then bear right to reach a few steps not far from the riverbank. Now simply follow the riverside path – the Dales Way in a north-to-south direction – to Hubberholme.

Hubberholme is a delightful spot. Its pub, the George Inn, is a long-standing venue for an annual land-letting ceremony held on the first Monday in each year, and which takes the form of an auction by candlelight at which bids are made for the use of a pasture owned by the church. The church itself is interesting, having been built as a forest chapel, and in 1241 given to the monks of Coverham Abbey.

At Hubberholme, pass round the church and over the Wharfe Bridge to turn left along the road, heading back towards Buckden. Before long, leave the road for a path on the left **D** which loops alongside the Wharfe, a safer option than walking down the road, which is very busy in summer. Eventually, the path does rejoin the road not far from Buckden Bridge, beyond which the village is only a short uphill stroll away. ●

# Sedbergh and Winder

| Start | Sedbergh |
|---|---|
| Distance | 7 miles (11.5km) |
| Approximate time | 4 hours |
| Parking | Loftus Hill, Sedbergh (free) |
| Refreshments | Pub and cafés in Sedbergh |
| Ordnance Survey maps | Landranger 97 (Kendal & Morecambe), Explorer OL19 (Howgill Fells & Upper Eden Valley) |

*Creating a bridge between the Pennines and the fells of Cumbria are the Howgills, which rise immediately to the north of Sedbergh. Their smooth, grassy, rounded slopes provide both excellent walking and dramatic scenery. This walk tackles one of the lower fells, Winder (pronounced to rhyme with 'bin'), which is easily if a little energetically accessible from Sedbergh. The route completes its circular tour by strolling along the banks of the River Rawthey using part of the Dales Way.*

From almost any point in the narrow streets of Sedbergh, the Howgills can be seen, their steep slopes presenting a dramatic backcloth to the town. Sedbergh is a small, stone-built town, and became part of Cumbria only in 1974, even though it remains in the Yorkshire Dales National Park, and clearly has many 'Dales' affinities. The town was formerly in the West Riding of Yorkshire, and is largely one long main street. It is an ancient market town with a charter dating from 1251, and is mentioned in the *Domesday Book* as among the many manors held by Earl Tostig of Northumbria. Today the fame of the town rests on the laurels of its school, set in parkland on the edge of the town. It was founded in 1525, and has grown steadily to earn a national reputation.

In spite of its administrative connections with Cumbria, Sedbergh remains one of the largest towns in the Yorkshire Dales National Park, and is the main western gateway to the Dales. The Turnpike Acts of 1761 brought improvements to the Askrigg–Kendal and Lancaster–Kirkby Stephen roads, both of which pass through Sedbergh, and these improvements made the town more accessible as a staging post for commercial routes across the Pennines. There followed a time of industrial growth as the domestic knitting trade was augmented by a cotton industry based on mills at Birks, Howgill and Millthrop.

The walk begins from the Loftus Hill car park near the church. Leave the car park and turn right, walking up to a T-junction near the Old Reading Room, now the public library. Turn left and then take the first on the right after the post office. The road rises gently and then continues, shortly going round a children's play area. Keep on towards a small housing estate on the upper edge

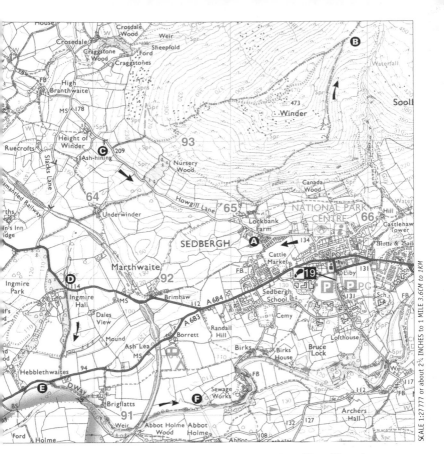

SCALE 1:27 777 or about 2¼ INCHES to 1 MILE 3.6CM to 1KM

of Sedbergh. Just past the houses, leave the road by turning right onto a narrow, hedgerowed lane (signposted Permissive Path to the fell) **A** that leads up to Lockbank Farm.

Go forward through a metal gate (waymarked) and up a broad walled track to a fell-gate. Through this turn left, climbing beside a wall. Almost immediately, leave the wallside path by ascending on the right, along a clear path crossing the hillside, climbing steeply. This shortly bears right and rises through bracken, in due course closing in on a small stream where it intercepts a broader, grassy track.

Turn right towards a shallow col ahead, beyond which the path continues rising at an easier angle across the southern slopes of Winder. Eventually it climbs to a small cairn beyond which it contours around the head of a valley on the right to reach another col **B** linking Winder with Arant Haw.

At the col, turn left having met up with another path. This now leads unerringly to the top of Winder, the summit marked by a triangulation pillar.

Leave the summit on the right-hand one of two ongoing grassy paths, which soon improves and eases steadily down the western ridge of Winder. Gradually, the descending path works down the side of the fell and comes to meet a wall not far from Nursery Wood. Turn right, alongside the wall for about 110 yds (100m), where a metal gate will be found to give onto a rough surfaced, enclosed track. Go down this to a surfaced lane (Howgill Lane). **C** Turn left, following the lane and taking care against approaching traffic as far as a stile beside a gate from where an ongoing footpath is signposted to Slacks Lane.

Go downfield beside a wall on the right, and a short way on passing above a stream gully to reach another stile beside a gate. Continue beyond this descending towards the buildings (mainly cottages/houses) at Underwinder, where another stile gives into house gardens, quickly crossed to another gate at the head of a surfaced lane. Head down the lane, later crossing a disused railway line, and following the lane down to a T-junction. Turn left to the main road (A684), and left again. *Take great care against approaching traffic*, and follow the road for 495 yds (450m), as far as the entrance to Ingmire Hall.

**D** Here, leave the road by turning right onto a signposted bridleway for the A683. Continue past cottages and onto a delightful, enclosed path along the boundary of Ingmire Hall estate. The wooded track leads down to a rough surface, which in turn runs out to the A683. Turn right for about 110 yds (100m), as far as a small lay-by on the left **E**, and there turn left through a metal kissing-gate (signposted to Birks Mill). Now following part of the Dales Way, head on to reach the banks of the River Rawthey, soon approaching the tiny settlement of Brigflatts.

Brigflatts was once a flax weavers' settlement. Here stands a Friends' Meeting House, a small and beautiful white cottage, built as a co-operative effort in 1675, making it the oldest meeting house in the north of England. The house was built when non-conformist meetings were illegal, and failure to attend parish church brought persecution. It is said that one local man never attended the Meeting House

services without taking his night cap against the possibility of being taken off to prison. One farmer, Alexander Hebblethwaite, was fined eight shillings for meeting here, an enormous sum, which he refused to pay, and forfeited his cow.

The path runs between a fence and the river, but at a gate enters a large pasture. Keep on, parallel with the river, reaching an old railway viaduct. Go left through a gate and climb to cross the trackbed, descending steps on the other side to walk along the edge of another riverside pasture to a kissing-gate directly above the confluence of the rivers Dee and Rawthey **F**. The gate gives into a lightly wooded area before entering another riverside pasture. On the far side, the path runs between a fence and the river, soon reaching the end of a surfaced lane near a small industrial site.

Keep forward along the lane, and continue past a group of cottages. Turn right onto the signposted Rawthey Way, which passes around a large house. As it does so, leave the obvious path, and go down towards the river, to gain, at a step-stile, the playing fields of Sedbergh School. Walk along the field edge, once more in company with the Rawthey.

Beyond the playing fields, the path eases briefly away from the river and climbs to a wall gap. From this go forward, keeping to the left of a ruined tower, and just beyond that, reaching the corner of woodland which, a short way farther on, it enters. The way through the wood is waymarked, and soon drops into a very narrow, walled passageway.

The path then continues above a steep drop to the river, and shortly leads to a gated gap-stile giving into a pasture, across which a path leads to the Sedbergh road. Turn left and walk into the village.  ●

# Clapham, Crummack Dale and Austwick

| | |
|---|---|
| **Start** | Clapham |
| **Distance** | 7 miles (11.5km). Shorter version 4½ miles (7.2km) |
| **Approximate time** | 3½ hours (2 hours for shorter version) |
| **Parking** | Clapham (Pay and Display) |
| **Refreshments** | Pubs and cafés in Clapham, pub at Austwick |
| **Ordnance Survey maps** | Landranger 98 (Wensleydale & Upper Wharfedale), Explorer OL2 (Yorkshire Dales – Southern & Western areas) |

*From the attractive village of Clapham, the walk begins by following one of the many walled lanes in this area before making a detour to visit the geological phenomenon known as the Norber Erratics. With superb views all round, the route continues into the remote Crummack Dale, a sweet, green retreat, nothing like so well-visited as other dales, before heading along more walled lanes to the village of Austwick and returning across fields to Clapham. The walk traverses some of the fine limestone scenery.*

Clapham is a village of especial delight, captivating and blessed with old bridges and waterfalls, white cottages, old stone houses and stands of ancient trees. It is a place of which charm is not so much a cliché as a way of life. Of its church, the earliest known mention is to what would have been a simple wooden structure, in 1160, when the vicar, Adam, was witness to a legal document. In 1318, following the Battle of Bannockburn, when much of the north of England was defenceless, raiding Scots burned down the church. In the Middle Ages, the replacement church was dedicated to St Michael, although the present structure, substantially rebuilt during the reign of George IV, is dedicated to St James the Apostle.

*Norber Erratic*

✏️ Leave the car park in Clapham, turn right up Gildersbank and go past the entrance to Ingleborough Hall Outdoor Education Centre. Ingleborough Hall was formerly the home of Reginald Farrer (1880–1920), a

*The way out of Clapham*

renowned botanist who, during the second half of his brief life, made repeated journeys to far corners of the world in pursuit of his passion, and brought many foreign plant specimens to Clapham to decorate the grounds of his home.

At the church, bear right and immediately left on a bridleway (signposted for Austwick). The route soon passes through the tunnels of the Ingleborough Estate, and then continues, climbing gently as a stony, walled track.

When the track divides, branch right onto an ancient packhorse route (Thwaite Lane) that linked Richmond and Lancaster. Follow this for ½ mile (800m), and then leave the walled track by branching left at a signpost **A**, and striking across fields for Norber. Head for a wall corner, and then follow the wall to a stile, then continuing directly below Robin Proctor's Scar, and finally climbing a little to reach a signpost **B**.

Looking east from the signpost, a jumble of boulders and low limestone cliffs is evident. The boulders and many more on the hillside above are the Norber Erratics, basically debris deposited here as the glaciers retreated at the end of the last Ice Age. Close inspection of the rocks will show them to be rather different from the surrounding limestone; they are in fact mostly of Silurian slate, which is a harder substance and more able to withstand the grinding effects of glaciers. Today they stand in splendid isolation; some are perched precariously on top of other smaller boulders.

From the signpost, follow the direction for Crummack, which takes a narrow path through boulders and, shortly after a stile, passes across the top of a limestone edge (Nappa Scars), which can be slippery when wet. Beyond, a clear path continues eastwards to meet a surfaced lane (Crummack Lane).

*Walkers wanting to omit the Crummack Dale section should turn right here and follow the lane down to Austwick, picking up the longer route there at the road junction just south of the Gamecock pub.*

Turn left. The surfacing, however, soon ends, and a delightful walled track continues to a junction with another

lane on the right (signposted for Wharfe). **C** Continue along this winding lane into the hamlet of Wharfe. Here, continue to follow the walled lane, now heading southwards, to reach another surfaced lane. Turn right for 150 yds (125m) and then at a signposted bridleway, leave the road by branching left **D** towards Wood End Farm, now following Wood Lane.

Just before the farm, bear right along another walled lane and follow this to a track junction. Here keep left, remaining on Wood Lane and follow this out to a road on the edge of Austwick. Turn right to the village crossroads. Turn left, past the church along the road for Clapham until you reach a gate and through-stile on the right (signposted 'Footpath to Clapham 2 miles') **E**. Here leave the road and continue up the ensuing field, following an obvious broad green track into a hummocky pasture, and cross to a ladder-stile and gap-stile. Cross the next field to a gated gap. Maintain the same direction in the next field to reach a ladder-stile in a wall corner, and then cross to another.

The way over the remaining fields takes an obvious route, linked by gates of one kind or another, and leads into the edge of Clapham. As the route approaches Clapham it is guided by a fence towards a farm. Near the farm the path is enclosed between barbed wire fences. At the farm, the path is waymarked and leads to a stile giving into the car park. ●

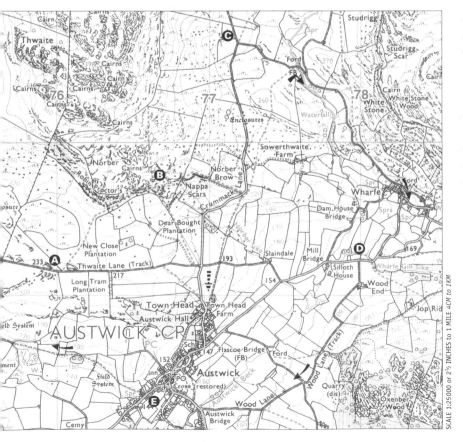

Giggleswick Scar and Stainforth Force

# Gsuggleswick Scar and Stainforth Force

| | |
|---|---|
| **Start** | Settle |
| **Distance** | 8¼ miles (13.3km) |
| **Approximate time** | 4–5 hours |
| **Parking** | Settle (Pay and Display) |
| **Refreshments** | Settle |
| **Ordnance Survey maps** | Landranger 98 (Wensleydale & Upper Wharfedale), Explorer OL41 (Forest of Bowland & Ribblesdale) |

*From the busy market town of Settle, the walk first climbs onto Giggleswick Scar before cutting across wild and open limestone moorland to the isolated hamlet of Feizor. The return leg explores yet more wide open spaces before dropping to Little Stainforth and the banks of the River Ribble. Stainforth Force provides a spectacular white water moment before the river relaxes and offers companionship all the way back to Settle.*

Like most larger market towns in the Dales, Settle lies on a river, the Ribble in this case, at a point where the narrow uplands of the dale broaden into a wider and greener valley. The Ribble, unlike most Dales' rivers, flows west into the Irish Sea instead of east to the North Sea. The town is a delightful mix of winding streets and small squares, and makes an excellent walking centre.

Leave the centre of Settle by turning down a pedestrianised side street opposite the town hall (signposted for the Friends' Meeting House), and go ahead beneath the railway line and forward past a supermarket, walking on as far as the fire station. Just before the fire station, turn left onto a surfaced pathway between a light industrial estate and housing. At the bottom of the pathway, bear right, passing around converted warehouses to locate a footbridge spanning the Ribble.

Cross the bridge, and bear half-left, uphill to a gate giving onto a walled passageway that emerges at the edge of Giggleswick. Turn right and walk to the end of Bankwell Road, there turning right and climbing steeply (Belle Hill) to meet the main road. Cross into The Mains opposite **Ⓐ**.

At the top end of The Mains, leave the housing behind by going forward onto an enclosed path, that wanders on easily and finally climbs to the upper edge of woodland at a ladder-stile.

Over the stile, turn immediately right on a path roughly parallel with a wall. After about 110 yds (100m), as the path forks, branch left, climbing across rough ground to run alongside the upper edge of a huge quarry. Keep on to pass the quarry, and then, beyond it, bear left, heading for a waymark pole and, farther on, a signpost. At the signpost **Ⓑ**, bear right onto a lovely

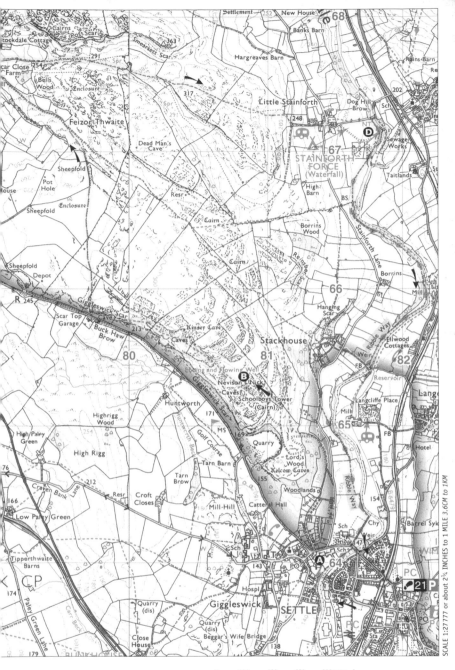

SCALE 1:27 777 or about 2¼ INCHES to 1 MILE 3.6CM to 1KM

path that goes forward along the edge of Giggleswick Scar.

After a wall gap, the path bears left, keeping below the uppermost level of the Scar. The path leads on to a ladder-stile and then continues to another about 330 yds (300m) distant. Over the second of these, keep forward on a clear path, roughly parallel with a wall at the escarpment edge. The path leads to a gate and finger-post. Beyond, bear half-right on a clear path heading out onto the limestone plateau.

*On the moors above Feizor*

The path takes a clear route across the plateau, linked by gates and ladder-stiles, and continues to another finger-post at the high point of the route, beyond which it descends as a broad grassy track to Feizor, there reaching a gate at the edge of the hamlet.

Go through the gate and down to a surfaced lane, turning right, following the road for a short distance before turning right over a ladder-stile **C**. Go forward (signposted for Stainforth) to a small gate and then keep ahead up a shallow rocky gully, and continuing along the right-hand side of a pasture, beside a wall. Just before the end of the field, cross another ladder-stile, and bear left, climbing gently.

The path rises steadily to a high point from which it heads forward across limestone moorland, on a broad grassy track, with the route clear throughout and linked by ladder-stiles.

The track offers lovely views of Ribblesdale and eventually descends to a gate just above Little Stainforth. Go down towards the buildings below, and on to a crossroads. Keep forward, and soon reach Stainforth Bridge **D**, an attractive packhorse bridge built in the 17th century.

Leave the road here by turning through a gap-stile to reach the true right bank of the Ribble, with the spectacular Stainforth Force only a short way ahead.

A clear path now parallels the river at varying distances from it, and continuing very agreeably as far as a footbridge. Here, ignore the bridge, and turn right up a walled lane to Stackhouse. At a T-junction, turn left along a lane, following this as far as a signposted gap-stile on the left, and taking care against approaching traffic.

Cross a field, and then resume a course much nearer to the river, gradually losing height until finally, at the edge of a playing field, the path once more touches upon the riverbank. A path now runs along the edge of the playing field to meet the main road at the edge of Settle. Turn left and walk back into town. ●

# Bolton Abbey, Barden Tower and The Strid

| | |
|---|---|
| **Start** | Bolton Abbey |
| **Distance** | 7½ miles (12km) |
| **Approximate time** | 4 hours |
| **Parking** | Bolton Abbey (seasonal charge) |
| **Refreshments** | Bolton Abbey, Barden Tower and Cavendish Pavilion |
| **Ordnance Survey maps** | Landranger 104 (Leeds & Bradford), Explorer OL2 (Yorkshire Dales – Southern & Western areas) |

*Bolton Abbey, or more accurately the remains thereof, have been the inspiration of many – poets, artists, photographers and authors generally. The ruins harmonise well with their setting amid meadow, moorland, woodland and the sinuous embrace of the River Wharfe, creating a scene of unrivalled beauty. A short distance up river, the Wharfe barges its way through a narrow rocky gorge, The Strid, while farther on it passes the ruins of Barden Tower. All these elements combine in this walk, which begins with a steady ascent onto moorland before heading for the river.*

The first part of the walk, across fields, woods and moorland, is easy to follow. From the car park walk out to the Burnsall road and turn left, and, soon after passing beneath an 18th-century arch (that was once an aqueduct), branch left onto a track signposted to Halton Heights **A**.

Follow the track for a short distance to a gate, and here bear right and across a field to a footpath sign near a fence corner and a pond. Follow the fence, and then cross to a gate, turning right in the ensuing field, stepping across a mid-field stream, to enter a wood. After a short climb, turn abruptly left at a signpost, and follow the ongoing path through the wood to a gate in a wall.

Now strike across the ensuing field to a gate in a wall, and from it maintain a similar direction, heading across another large pasture and aiming for another gate about 30 yds (27m) to the east of a wall corner **B**.

Through the gate, turn left to follow a path parallel with a wall on the left to the col between Little and Middle Hare Head, where the path rises onto the latter. Continue across this minor summit to a gate in a wall, and a few strides farther on, leave the main path by branching right **C** to descend through heather and then bracken to a gate beside the road below. Ignore the gate, but continue alongside the wall to another gate lower down, just above a wall corner. Through this, turn right and follow the road to a T-junction with the B6160. There turn left and walk down to Barden Tower.

Barden Tower used to belong to the Clifford family, whose main stronghold was Skipton Castle. It was originally built in the 12th century as a hunting lodge, but was rebuilt and extended in the 15th century, and it is the ruins of this later building that remain today.

From the tower, leave the B6160 by branching right down the road for Appletreewick, walking as far as Barden Bridge and, just before the bridge **D**, turn right, through a wall gap and down steps to join a riverside path. The remaining section, largely shared with the Dales Way, simply follows the river and is quite delightful.

Shortly after passing a turreted bridge – a Victorian aqueduct carrying water to Bradford – keep on across meadows to a gate giving into Strid

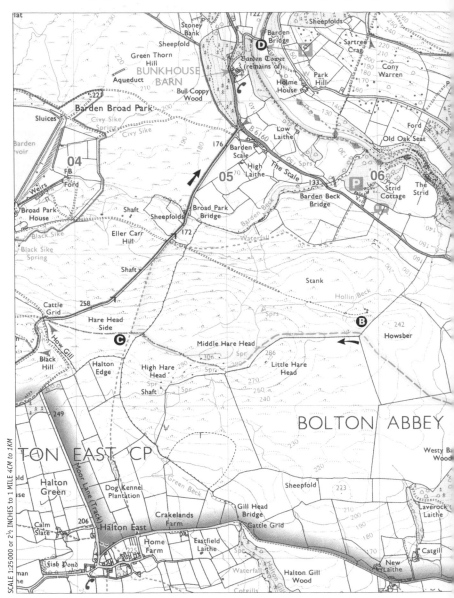

Woods. The woodland is owned by the Devonshire Estates and a small charge is usually levied to walk through them.

Although there are a number of paths through the woodland – and with time you could easily explore more – this walk follows the path closest to the river. *During wet conditions some parts of the path can be slippery.*

Eventually, the path reaches the narrowing known as The Strid, where the cascading water is usually heard long before it is seen. At one point here the river is only a few yards wide and surges through the gap with tremendous force: *this is not a place to attempt any heroics by trying to leap across the river – quite a few people have died here hoping to do just that.*

Strid Wood is renowned for its flora

Bolton Abbey

and fauna. Almost all of the trees are broad-leaved, some as much as 300 years old. There are at least 60 species of nesting birds here and over 80 species of lichen.

After The Strid the path is a little easier, and broadens out into a flat and well-defined track that eventually works a way onward to Cavendish Pavilion, beside which the river is crossed by a footbridge. On the other side, turn right to a stile and there turn left by Pickles Beck. Cross a minor road (Hazlewood Lane) and walk uphill for a short distance to a signposted path on the right for Bolton Abbey.

The path winds agreeably through riverside woodland, eventually dropping to a broad grassy expanse formed by a river loop. Ahead lies another Wharfe bridge, beyond which stand the ruins of Bolton Priory. Across the bridge follow a clear path up to a flight of steps leading up to a 'hole' in a wall. *Take care emerging onto the road beyond.* Cross with care and go ahead to return to the visitor centre and car park.

Bolton Priory was founded in 1154 and dissolved in 1539, one of the last among Henry VIII's Dissolution of the Monasteries to fall. Part of the structure, however, survives and is still used as the local church. The surrounding priory buildings have almost entirely disappeared, apart from the gatehouse, which is incorporated into the present, mainly Victorian, Bolton Hall. ●

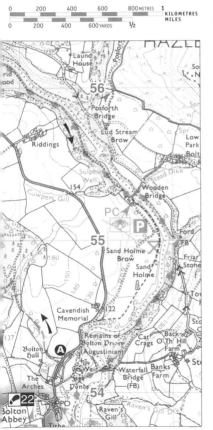

# Pateley Bridge and Brimham Rocks

| | |
|---|---|
| **Start** | Pateley Bridge |
| **Distance** | 9 miles (14.5km) |
| **Approximate time** | 5 hours |
| **Parking** | Car park beside the bridge in Pateley Bridge. Toilets across the road. |
| **Refreshments** | Pateley Bridge, self-service kiosk at Brimham Rocks |
| **Ordnance Survey maps** | Landranger 99 (Northallerton & Ripon), Explorer 298 (Nidderdale) |

*This delightful walk takes an elevated route out of Pateley Bridge, offering lovely views as it heads towards Brimham Rocks. From the rocks, the walk heads for Smelthouses, eventually reaching the River Nidd, alongside which it returns to the start.*

Of all the Dales, Nidderdale is the least well-known nationally – though local walkers have enjoyed its pleasures for years. It was excluded from the Yorkshire Dales National Park, but did later receive some protection when it was created an Area of Outstanding Natural Beauty. Pateley Bridge, where this walk begins, is a busy Dales town on the banks of the River Nidd, and gets its name from the river crossing first used by the monks of Fountains Abbey. Lead mining, quarrying and to a lesser extent textiles were all important in the history of Pateley Bridge, though today the economy is largely based on agriculture and tourism.

Leave Pateley Bridge by walking up High Street and at the top turning right with the main road into Ripon Road to go past the Methodist church. A short way farther on, leave the road by turning left up steps onto the signposted Panorama Walk. A surfaced path climbs between walls, with steadily improving views across the dale, until it reaches a track junction

at Bishopdale. Here, keep left, still climbing between walls to another junction, where road surfacing begins. Keep forward, now descending gently, the route signposted for Blazefield.

As the road bends right, leave it by branching left onto a vehicle track (signposted as the Nidderdale Way). After passing a cottage the track deteriorates to an overgrown path. When it forks, bear right, descending and eventually emerging at a road. Turn left and walk up towards the terraced houses of Blazefield.

After about 220 yds (200m), as the first houses are reached, leave the road by branching right onto a continuation of the Nidderdale Way **Ⓐ**, which runs along the terrace, and then starts to descend as a rough vehicle track. With the added height gain since leaving Pateley Bridge, the view across the dale is even better.

At a minor road, turn right, leaving the Nidderdale Way and descending for about 110 yds (100m) to a signposted path on the left for Wilsill. Turn left here, through two metal gates and then from a third gate keep forward across a grassy slope, and later bearing left to a wooden gate in a field corner. Through the gate keep forward through another and along the top edge of two sloping pastures, walking beside a wall to a final gate giving onto a lane at Raikes.

Cross into a narrow enclosed path opposite sandwiched between buildings to meet a step-stile from which keep forward to a gated gap and then cross to another gate. Shortly beyond the gate a through-stile on the right crosses into an adjacent field. Over this go half-left to a gap stile, and then continue across the next field following a wall on the right and then keeping forward to another gate. Cross the top of an access track to a nearby cottage, to a narrow gap-stile and wooden gate, and then bear left alongside a wall to a complex wall junction. Maintain the same direction, going forward towards light woodland and a field corner gate.

Through the gate, turn left onto a rough track, and immediately left again onto a waymarked bridleway between

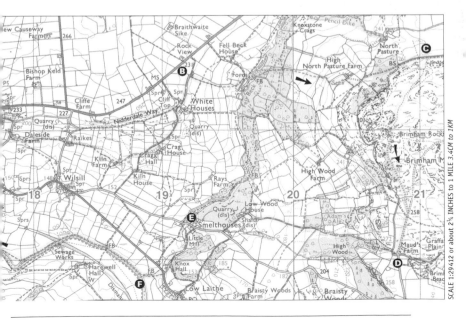

overgrown walls. Continue to a track junction at White Houses and then go forward onto a bridleway signposted for Ripon Road, having now rejoined the Nidderdale Way. Keep going as far as a row of cottages and a signposted footpath on the right for Brimham Rocks **B**. Turn right here along an enclosed path to a stile.

The ongoing route downfield is waymarked and provides a fine view across to Brimham Rocks. It leads through a wall gap towards another track junction just at the edge of the wooded gorge that contains Fell Beck. From the junction bear right on a waymarked footpath that leads to a footbridge spanning the beck.

From the footbridge, keep slightly left to follow a fence, leaving the woodland and climbing steadily over stiles and generally keeping to the left-hand edge of a number of fields, eventually heading for High North Pasture Farm. Keep to the right of the farm, using its access track for a short while, before heading into an area of light woodland.

The ongoing track later bears left towards a road, but about 165 yds (150m) before it does so, leave it by turning south **C** and take a lovely path through heather and rough moorland up towards Brimham Rocks.

There are many paths across the moorland, and which you take is irrelevant – the general direction is south, but time should be taken to explore this fantastic landscape. The rocks are a series of gritstone boulders that have become fashioned by time and weather into shapes that have inevitably attracted fanciful names from Victorian visitors – the Dancing Bear, the Anvil, the Sphinx. This whole area is owned by the National Trust, who have provided an information centre and shop, as well as a car park, and it is the car park which eventually

becomes the objective. From it begins the return journey to Pateley Bridge.

Continue to a T-junction and there turn right along a surfaced lane for about 330 yds (300m), as far as a signpost **D** for Smelthouses. Take the right-hand one of two gates ahead and follow a grassy path below a low cliff which winds attractively downhill through woodland and across fields towards Low Wood House. Here bear left to reach a main road, and turn right towards Smelthouses.

**E** On reaching Smelthouses, turn left, just before Fell Beck bridge onto a signposted bridleway, a stony track that leads past old mill buildings converted to houses and soon rejoins Fell Beck as it passes along the edge of more light woodland. The track comes down to pass through another group of buildings to reach the road at Low Laithe.

Cross onto a path opposite signposted for Glasshouses and follow a field path to a wall corner where a stile gives onto a narrow path leading to a footbridge for the last crossing of Fell Beck. A short distance farther on, Fell Beck meets its confluence with the River Nidd.

**F** Turn right to walk up river, crossing an in-flowing stream on stepping stones. The riverside vegetation is understandably lush and includes alder, rowan, ash, birch, sycamore and the invasive Indian balsam. With only minor deviations, keep going until the path is deflected right through a small light industrial estate at Glasshouses.

Emerging at a road, turn left and just before reaching the Nidd bridge, turn right onto a signposted path, a broad track between low walls that soon reaches a large reservoir. The track continues past a weir, and then becomes a surfaced path along the banks of the river, leading unerringly back into Pateley Bridge.

# Jervaulx Abbey and Middleham

| | |
|---|---|
| **Start** | Jervaulx Abbey |
| **Distance** | 9¼ miles (15km) |
| **Approximate time** | 5 hours |
| **Parking** | Opposite entrance to Jervaulx Abbey (honesty box) |
| **Refreshments** | Café at Jervaulx Abbey, pub at East Witton, pubs and cafés in Middleham, pub at Cover Bridge |
| **Ordnance Survey maps** | Landranger 99 (Northallerton & Ripon), Explorers 302 (Northallerton & Thirsk) and OL30 (Yorkshire Dales – Northern & Central areas) |

*Many of the Yorkshire Dales have an abbey and castle reasonably close to each other and which can be linked by attractive footpaths. Wensleydale is no exception, and this outstanding walk through the wide, green and gentle lower part of the dale links the stark ruins of Middleham Castle with the mellowed stone walls of Jervaulx Abbey.*

🖊 Leave the car path and turn right, following the roadside for 330 yds (300m), *taking care against approaching traffic especially near a blind rise.* Take the first turning on the right, a side lane (Newstead Lanc), signposted for Ellingstring and Healey. Stay on the road as it bends left at Low Newstead Farm, and continue for another ½ mile (800m) as far as a broad farm access (Hammer Lane) on the right. Leave the road here, and follow the access to Hammer Farm with improving views to the right over Wensleydale.

At the farm, keep to the left of the buildings, following a waymarked route through to a gate at the back of the farm buildings, giving into a small paddock **Ⓐ**. Through the gate cross to the far corner of the paddock, where another gate gives onto a short track flanked by a narrow strip of woodland.

In the ensuing pasture, turn right following a constructed track alongside the woodland and following the field boundary to a metal gate. Through this, turn right to another gate a few strides farther on and continue to follow the track as it descends a sloping pasture, passes another gate at the bottom, and then bears right towards Thirsting Castle Lodge **Ⓑ**.

At a track junction, turn left to pass the lodge and soon reach the top end of a surfaced lane that leads delightfully all the way down to the lovely village of East Witton. Turn left and walk up alongside the extended village green. At the far end of the green, take the road on the right, but for only about 90 yds (80m), as far as a signposted footpath on the right turning into a field **Ⓒ**. In the field, go immediately left alongside a fence and intermittent hedgerow to reach another stile at the left-hand edge of a short section of wall.

In the ensuing field, cross to the far right-hand corner, and through a stile cross another narrow pasture to gain a rough lane (West Field Lane). Keep forward along this, and where the lane ends at a field gate, turn left through an adjacent gate giving into the edge of a narrow strip of woodland. Follow the ongoing path, which later swings round to a step-stile giving into the corner of a large arable field. Turn left along the edge of the woodland and soon reach a dilapidated stone wall. Walk alongside the wall and continue into the next field, now following a field edge vehicle track which, farther on, passes into the adjacent field and immediately resumes the same direction to a gate. Keep forward in the pasture beyond, alongside a hedge and fence.

As the field boundary dog-legs to the right, cut across to a metal gate **D**, and through this follow the left-hand field edge into the next field, continuing in the same direction to reach a step-stile and footbridge. Over the bridge, bear left alongside a post-and-wire fence, but soon start drifting away from the fence, half-right, to locate a gated gap-stile beside a wooden gate and small storage hut in a dip **E**. Cross to another gate, and then keep left along the top edge of a slope above the River Cover.

Follow a clear path which eventually swings round to descend to a bridge (Hullo Bridge) spanning the river. Over the bridge, climb briefly alongside a wall, and, near a wall corner, go through a gated gap-stile on the right, and strike across the ensuing pasture on a clear

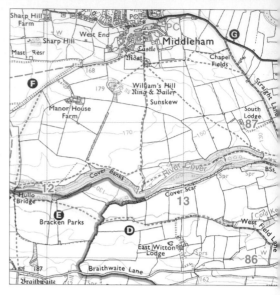

path that leads out to meet a road (Coverham Lane) **F**. Racehorses are often exercised on the heath opposite.

Turn right and follow the road down into Middleham, passing the gaunt ruins of 12th-century Middleham Castle, for two centuries one of the strongholds of the powerful Neville family, the earls of Warwick.

Middleham is little more than a large village, but a charming one at that, with some imposing Georgian houses and a good stock of inns and tearooms to accommodate the jaded traveller.

Leave Middleham along the Masham road (A6108), but after 650 yds (600m) leave it by turning right onto a broad, walled track (Straight Lane) **G**. When the track bears right leave it by continuing forward along an enclosed footpath that soon leads into the corner of a large pasture. Maintain the same direction, now alongside a wall, and soon descend to the banks of the River Cover. Turn left to locate a narrow stile in a wall corner giving onto a splendid riverside path (waymarked) flanked in springtime by wild ransome, celandine,

SCALE 1:27777 or about 2¼ INCHES to 1 MILE 3.6CM to 1KM

bluebell, butterbur, wood anemone and meadow cranesbill.

After ½ mile (800m), the path is steered away from the river to reach the A-road near the Cover Bridge Inn. Turn right, passing the inn, and crossing the Cover Bridge. On the other side, leave the road by turning left through a kissing-gate to gain a signposted path setting off as a grassy track alongside a hedgerow but later continuing along the top of flood banks. The adjacent River Cover soon joins the Ure **H**, which then makes an idyllic companion for the next mile (2km).

In the end, the riverside track meets a gate and is turned out to rejoin the A6108. At the road, go left and soon return to the car park at Jervaulx.

The abbey at Jervaulx dates from 1156, and, like all the monasteries in the Yorkshire Dales and elsewhere, grew rich from the proceeds of sheep farming, but, almost prophetically, they also excelled at making cheese and breeding horses, two of today's most successful enterprises in Wensleydale. The ruins today are a sorry sight, and the result of the wrath of Henry VIII who had particular cause to be displeased by the last abbot, Adam Sedbar; as a result Jervaulx was more mutilated than the other monasteries in Yorkshire, and much of the stone has long since disappeared into other buildings in the area.

●

# Garsdale Head and Hell Gill

| Start | Garsdale Head, near Garsdale station |
|---|---|
| Distance | 8 miles (12.7km) |
| Approximate time | 4–5 hours |
| Parking | Limited roadside parking along the station road |
| Refreshments | Moorcock Inn, Garsdale Head |
| Ordnance Survey maps | Landranger 98 (Wensleydale & Upper Wharfedale) and Explorer OL19 (Howgill Fells & Upper Eden Valley) |

*This is a demanding walk that visits an area of open moorland between Garsdale and Upper Wensleydale. There is a keen sense of isolation, and the bleakness of the moors lends appeal and exhilaration to the walk. On some stretches there is no discernible footpath, and in other places only a wet trod across rough hill pasture.* A lack of identifiable landmarks makes this a walk for a clear and warm day: it should not be attempted otherwise. Take plenty of refreshments and warm clothing.

From the roadside parking, walk down to the valley road, and cross to a gated gap-stile opposite the T-junction. Through this, take to a footpath signposted for Grisedale and Flust which begins by climbing gently, roughly parallel with a wall on the left. At first, the path is quite broad, and boggy – a hallmark of much of this walk, except after a prolonged dry spell – but this is soon left by branching left onto an intermittent and narrow path across rough ground. The path aims for a gap-stile about 33 yds (30m) to the right of a gate.

The ongoing path is signposted and treks across open moorland, wet and boggy, but nothing, compared with the vertical quagmire that is the huge lump of Baugh Fell, the dominating hill to the west. The path climbs steadily to reach the edge of a steep-sided ravine containing Grisedale Beck, where it follows the rim of the ravine to another wall and gated gap-stile. Through this continue across open moorland, and later keeping to the right of the cottage at Blake Mire to reach a stile beside a field gate. In the ensuing field, bear half-right through tussock grass and reed to a collapsed gap-stile in a wall to the left of a field barn, and then go forward across the next field to another stile (signposted) looking down on a group of farm buildings and Grisedale Road.

Descend to a derelict farm building (Rowantree, on the right) and there pass through another gap-stile giving onto a field track. Keep ahead across a pasture, aiming to the left of a field barn. Go through a nearby gate and across the next field, heading for a row of cottages, and there join surfaced Grisedale Road.

Ⓐ Turn right onto the road and follow it to East House, there climbing steadily through a gate. Shortly, the ascending lane swings right and, a little farther on, bears round to the left. Leave the lane here, by branching right onto a rough track beside a wall. Follow this for no more than 165 yds (150m), and then leave it by bearing left across wet and trackless moorland of Grisedale Common, heading roughly in a north-easterly direction onto Turner Hill, a far flung outlier of the bulky Swarth Fell, away to the left.

*This is no place to be in poor visibility or adverse weather conditions.* The absence of either reliable landmarks or paths puts reliance on navigational skills, though there is a saving grace in the form of a wall and fence along the highpoint of the moor, which marks the county boundary between North Yorkshire and Cumbria. If you intersect the wall, turn left; if you meet a fence, turn right. Where wall and fence meet, there is a gate, the key to the onward route.

**B** Through the gate, go forward alongside a descending wall on the right. Lower down, as the wall bears to the right, leave the accompanying path by branching left, once more onto trackless moorland, above the upper reaches of Wensleydale. Route-finding is now not easy, and the ground rough to negotiate. In the valley below, the road, the Settle–Carlisle railway line and the farm buildings at Shaw Paddock soon come into view. Stay high on the valley sides until the derelict farm at High Shaw Paddock appears, and then head towards it. A waymarked gap-stile is encountered first, with the farm a short distance ahead across an enclosed intake field.

**C** Pass in front of the farm buildings to a gate. Through this, cross a stream and then bear right to follow a wall on the right. Shortly, go through a gate at a wall corner, and continue, still alongside a wall.

The ongoing path, such as it is, heads through another gate, and from this keep forward across a neck of land and shortly rejoin the wall. Just before the wall ends another gate takes the route onwards. When the wall does end, not far from the road, continue forward parallel with a fence, and soon, on the county boundary, go through a gate and walk to the road.

Cross with care into the wide track opposite (signposted for Hell Gill and Helm Gill), soon crossing the Settle–Carlisle railway line, after which the track bends left. Just before Hellgill Force and the River Eden, turn right, still on the track, and follow this, soon crossing the Eden, and walking up to Hellgill cottage. Keep past the cottage, now following a broad, grassy track to a gate at Hell Gill Bridge, where the High Way is encountered. Turn right, through a gate and cross the bridge.

**D** Now follow the High Way, a wide, grassy path across moorland, and when it forks after about 220 yds (200m), branch left. Soon, a significant piece of ground is crossed. Between Hell Gill and the next significant stream – which turns out to be the infant River Ure – the route crosses the watershed of Britain. The waters of the Ure, rising on the slopes of Lunds Fell, flow through Wensleydale and east to the North Sea. Those of the Eden flow west into the Solway Firth.

The track leads on to the ruins of High Hall Farm, just before which a ford needs to be crossed. On reaching the farm buildings **E**, go through two dilapidated wooden gates at the gable end, to reach a sloping pasture. Bear obliquely left, targeting a distant plantation, crossing trackless ground. Shortly, pass through a wall gap and cross another sloping field to a gap-stile to the right of a gate, and then follow a narrow path descending diagonally to

another wall gap with a stile beside it. Through this keep parallel to a wall, descending towards a barn.

Before the barn is reached, go through a gate and descend left to cross a stream, and then head for the barn. Go past the barn and over a gap-stile in the wall to the left of a gate. Continue with the descending track to another gate and gap-stile below a stand of conifers. Now go down to a wall junction below those conifers, and there take the right-hand gate (metal) of two gates. Turn left beside a wall as far as a gap-stile about 55 yds (50m) distant. Over this, strike across rough pasture to another gap-stile and gate, beyond which a track runs on to a gate at a farm access and near farm buildings. Cross the access, and go into the next field, crossing to a footbridge spanning a gill to reach the redundant 18th-century Lunds Chapel-of-Ease.

**F** Turn right in front of the chapel (signposted for the B6259), and walk down to a gate giving back onto the farm access. Turn left to cross a footbridge spanning the River Ure, and immediately head forward into Lunds Plantation, following a broad track. As the track starts to bear gently to the right, keep an eye open for a stile and signpost (The Quarry and B6259) on the left, where the right of way plunges boggily into the plantation.

The interior of the plantation is dense and dark, but the way through, while not easy to follow, is confirmed by the presence of three small footbridges. Finally, daylight appears ahead as the path reaches the plantation edge. Turn right alongside a wall for about 33 yds (30m), and then cross through a gap-stile on the left, and bear diagonally right across the ensuing field to another

stile about 44 yds (40m) to the right of a gated wall corner. Cut across the corner of the next field to another gap-stile to the left of a gate, and through this bear half-right to a signposted stile giving onto the B-road.

Turn left, and walk along the roadside, *taking care against approaching traffic*, for about 440 yds (400m), and leave the road, opposite the cottage at South Lund **G**, by turning right at a stile onto a footpath signposted to East Mudd (sic) Becks. Head towards the railway footbridge ahead, and on the other side, go through a narrow, gated stile in a corner, giving into rough pasture. Bear half-right down the pasture, heading for a collapsed wall. A wet, but discernible path leads across the pasture and continues climbing above the wall.

The route now once more lies across featureless moorland, but there is narrow grassy path across it. The path climbs steadily, but on reaching a high point drifts off to the left. At this point, leave it, and cross, right, to a wall spanned by a tall ladder-stile (broken step on the far side at the time of writing). Over this, continue on a gently rising path across more rough pasture, and targeting Garsdale station, which has now come into view.

The path is muddy, and leads to a gap-stile. Through this the path descends across more pasture. Keep heading for the station, and when you cannot see this, target the conspicuous cairn on the fell beyond. Eventually, the path leads through a tumbledown wall, after which it goes down across more rough pasture, aiming for the right-hand edge of a row of cottages at the valley road.

At the road, cross through a gated stile, and follow the road back to the turning to Garsdale station and the conclusion of the walk.

0   200   400   600   800 METRES   1
                                    KILOMETRES
                                    MILES
0   200   400   600 YARDS   ½

# Pen-y-ghent

| | |
|---|---|
| **Start** | Horton-in-Ribblesdale |
| **Distance** | 5½ miles (9km) |
| **Height gain** | 455m (1493 feet) |
| **Approximate time** | 2–3 hours |
| **Parking** | Horton-in-Ribblesdale (Pay and Display) |
| **Refreshments** | Pen-y-Ghent Café nearby, and pubs in Horton |
| **Ordnance Survey maps** | Landranger 98 (Wensleydale & Upper Wharfedale), Explorer OL2 (Yorkshire Dales – Southern & Western areas) |

*Like an ancient galleon, Pen-y-ghent's two-tiered prow sails purposefully across the surrounding countryside, drawing thousands to its summit each year. The hill is the lowest of the Yorkshire 'Three Peaks', but makes up for it by being the only one to entertain the Pennine Way. It lies barely two miles (3.2km) by crow from the valley of the Ribble which it overlooks, and its ascent need occupy little more than half a day.*

Opinions differ as to the meaning and origin of the name, Pen-y-ghent, which despite a once strong Norman influence in the valley below, must derive from the Celtic, from the Kingdom of Brigantia and the tribes forced into what were then remote regions by Roman and Teutonic settlers. Generally thought to mean 'Hill of the Winds', but believed by others to mean 'Hill of the Border Country', its name unquestionably comes from the Welsh language, rendered *Pen y Gwynt* and *Pen y Cant* respectively, – *cant* meaning a rim.

🥾 The walk begins in the straggling village of Horton-in-Ribblesdale, mentioned as a farming community in the *Domesday Book* (1086–87), and to which King Henry VI came during the Wars of the Roses (1455–85) to hide from his enemies.

From the car park turn right to a track on the left leaving the road just past the Pen-y-ghent Café, and follow the signposted Pennine Way, which despite heading north east is, in fact, the southbound route. A steady amble of over a mile (2km) along the walled path leads easily to the fell gate, with

Pen-y-ghent looming large to the right. This route, Horton Scar Lane, is part of an ancient packhorse road once used to cross to Littondale.

Horton Scar Lane is easy walking, gaining height almost imperceptibly. On the right, a dry valley is a reminder of the underground drainage system which permeates these hills. Above all this, at the fell-gate **A** the route turns sharply right, but another prominent track continues ahead to Hull Pot, a great square-cut hole which looks almost as if it is man-made. The pot is only 330 yds (300m) beyond the gate, so it is worth a few minutes to make the diversion. In dry weather no water enters the pot, but when it is wet, with upstream sinks constricted, the resulting waterfall in Hull Pot is a splendid sight. Despite its massive size, there are times, perhaps only once or so each year, when the pot

fills up completely. Normally all the water sinks beneath the boulders, but this route, too, is constricted so that in times of full flood the water overflows down the dry valley.

By way of contrast, return to the fell-gate and pursue the path which leads steadily upwards to the rim of Pen-y-ghent, a direct and conspicuous route to the edge of the escarpment, where it turns abruptly right, and eases along the edge before a final short scamper to the summit. The view is now quite expansive, typical of the fine airy panoramas for which the Pennines are justly famous.

A wall crosses the summit of Pen-y-ghent, and just over it a triangulation pillar and a large cairn mark the highest ground. Immediately in front of them the path heads right to the prominent tiered southern end of the mountain,

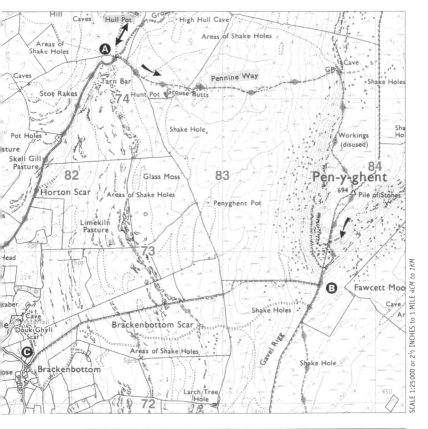

where the easy path abruptly ends. A rocky descent now follows, in the first of two stages. Neither is especially difficult, except perhaps in winter conditions, but hands, feet and bottoms are often employed here.

The second rock step has a narrow path running along the edge, and this despite its proximity to the rolling hillside has a more secure feel about it than nearby rocks, which are quite slippery when wet. In a matter of minutes, below all the rockwork, a couple of stiles are encountered on the right **B**. Here, leave the Pennine Way, cross the stiles and begin the long but easy and enjoyable descent to Brackenbottom.

**C** Turn right on reaching the minor road at Brackenbottom, and follow this out to arrive in a short while on the main valley road, near St Oswald's Church. The church dates from about 100, but has seen restoration work in 1400, when the tower was added, 1823 and 1879, as well as in modern times.

The car park is now only a few minutes away along the road.

*Pen-y-ghent*

# Ingleborough

| | |
|---|---|
| **Start** | Clapham |
| **Distance** | 10½ miles (17km) |
| **Height gain** | 1840 ft (560m) |
| **Approximate time** | 5 hours |
| **Parking** | Clapham (Pay and Display) |
| **Refreshments** | Clapham |
| **Ordnance Survey maps** | Landranger 98 (Wensleydale & Upper Wharfedale), Explorer OL2 (Yorkshire Dales – Southern & Western areas) |

*A fine walk of no great difficulty (unless you fall into Gaping Gill) beginning in a charming village, and taking in meltwater ravines, potholes, wild, moorland wandering, a high mountain summit, and dramatic limestone scenery. There are other ascents of Ingleborough, but this is undoubtedly the best.*

Clapham is a village of rare delight, captivating at every turn of the road, tastefully decorated with old bridges and waterfalls, white cottages, old stone houses and stands of ancient trees. It is a place of which 'rural charm' is not so much a cliché as a way of life, a place with a comfortable atmosphere of peace and tranquility. Weekends, as happens throughout the Yorkshire Dales, inject an element of fretting and fraying as visitors trip in to revitalise their jaded weekday spirits.

Viewed from the south west, Ingleborough rises as an isolated summit from an extensive plateau of limestone culminating in a fine series of scars overlooking Chapel-le-Dale. Once thought to have been the highest summit in England, the mountain has a unique appeal, its great sprawl dominating the countryside of west Craven, its distinctive flat-topped summit a feature easily identifiable from as far away as the western fells of Lakeland. Unspectacular in mountaineering terms, the vast Ingleborough landscape is nonetheless remarkable, its diverse nooks and crannies an immense store of botanical and archaeological goodies, its geological infrastructure a honeycomb of delight.

Begin by leaving the car park and moving right to cross Clapham Beck by an old stone bridge. Turn right and walk past a variety of cottages and the fine church of St James, substantially rebuilt in 1814, though its tower dates from the 14th century.

There is an option, soon encountered, of visiting the landscaped grounds of Ingleborough Hall Estate, but this walk continues past the entrance and shortly turns right into Clapdale Lane (signposted: 'Ingleborough; Gaping Gill: Ingleborough Cave'). Follow this easily as far as Clapdale Farm where a sharp descent, right, back towards the beck meets up with the path through the estate grounds. **A** Turn left, heading upstream.

Farther along Clapham Beck there are guided tours into Ingleborough Cave. In the early years of the 19th century the underground network of caverns between Gaping Gill and Clapham Beck Head remained a source of mystery and wonder. Ingleborough Cave, the obvious entrance, was blocked after only a few metres by a wall of stalagmite beyond which a tiny space of air stretched above a pool of water into the darkness. Occasional floods suggested that this cave might be connected to the underground river of Gaping Gill, and so in 1837 the landowner ordered the stalagmite barrier to be broken down, to drain away the lake it held back, and to allow exploration of the interior. A fine cavern was found part of the way to Gaping Gill, but it took almost another 150 years of spasmodic exploration before the final link was made.

Continue past the cave, and through a sheltered glen between low scars of limestone. Ahead, the main valley curves to the left and a stile gives into the rocky maw of Trow Gill, a classic example of a limestone gorge, built by a surface stream of meltwater flowing off the limestone plateau above

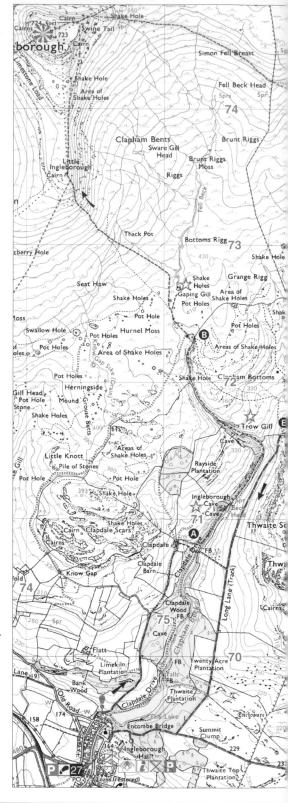

ease the waters of Fell Beck as they gather from the high grounds of Ingleborough. This wide open hole, of obviously great depth, was an irresistible challenge to the explorers of the 19th century, but it was not until the last decade of the century that a Frenchman, Edouard Martel, in August 1895, finally reached the floor of the shaft, more than 300ft (100m) down. The main chamber of Gaping Gill is the largest cavern in Britain, 460ft (140m) long and almost 100ft (30m) high and wide.

From Gaping Gill a path heads north west for the base of Little Ingleborough which is gained by a steepish pull to a bevy of shelter-cairns on its upper edge from where there is a fine prospect across Ribblesdale to Pen-y-ghent and Fountains Fell. Continue along a constructed path, rising in two geological 'steps' formed by the outcropping Yoredale Facies that give Ingleborough its distinctive profile, to gain the edge of the summit plateau. The summit shelter and triangulation pillar are not instantly visible, but soon come into view, along with Whernside, which together with Pen-y-ghent and Ingleborough make up the Yorkshire 'Three Peaks'.

The top of Ingleborough holds the remains of a hillfort, with a massive encircling wall, now collapsed, around the edge of a summit plateau, also containing the foundations, still traceable in the peaty summit, of 19

as the glaciers retreated at the end of the last Ice Age. Rising steadily the gorge is overlooked by slopes becoming higher and steeper, until it narrows dramatically to a spill of boulders over which walkers must clamber to reach the dry, grassy valley beyond.

The path now follows the line of a wall to a couple of adjacent ladder-stiles **B** (ignore an earlier single stile), beyond which lies the broad limestone plinth of Ingleborough. The onward route is now obvious. When the path forks, bear right to visit Gaping Gill.

Gaping Gill takes its name from its great entrance, which swallows with

*Pen-y-ghent from Sulber*

circular huts believed to be a settlement of the first Iron Age man in this district. It was from this elevated vantage point, named Rigodunum, that the Brigantian leader, Venutius, led a revolt against the Romans which was not finally quelled until AD74, by Julius Agricola.

The highest point, the true summit, is marked by a cairn on a rocky plinth a few metres north west of the triangulation pillar, and overlooks the Doe Valley. This has a history of its own, being the site of a round tower (a hospice) built in 1830, but substantially destroyed on the day of its opening by participants rather the worse for drink: the curved stones which formed its base are still clearly seen.

The onward descent leaves the north east corner of the summit plateau to gain a path along the southern flank of Simon Fell to a derelict shooting hut **C**. Beyond lies a weird landscape known as Sulber Scars, a massive desert of fissured white limestone through which a path picks its way to a lonely signpost at GR778735. Horton-in-Ribblesdale lies not far ahead, but here the route turns right on a grassy path to reach a stile at Sulber Gate.

**D** Continue ahead, keeping the wall on the left and when the path forks at a cairn a short distance farther on, keep right, making for the conspicuous cairn atop Long Scar. Later, before reaching Long Scar, another cairn marks a change of direction, again right, to enter a wide grassy amphitheatre known as Clapham Bottoms. The path is clear enough and leads via one gate to another at the head of Long Lane **E**, an old bridleway connecting Clapham and Selside in Ribblesdale.

A short way down Long Lane there is a fine view of Trow Gill, its naked limestone walls contrasting with the moulded grassy slopes of glacial moraine to its right. There are splendid views, too, across woodlands below in which shelters the village of Clapham, while a conspicuous dip in the lane marks the line of the North Craven Fault.

Long Lane eventually meets Thwaites Lane at a T-junction. Turn right into Thwaite Lane and descend towards Clapham, passing through two tunnels built by the Farrers to protect the privacy of their estate. This tunnelled lane ends near Clapham church at the top end of the village, from where the car park lies only a short distance away to the left. ●

# Gunnerside, Kisdon and Muker

| | |
|---|---|
| **Start** | Gunnerside |
| **Distance** | 10½ miles (16.5km) or 5½ miles (9km) |
| **Approximate time** | 5½ hours or 2½ hours |
| **Parking** | Gunnerside |
| **Refreshments** | Café and pub at Gunnerside; cafés and pub in Muker |
| **Ordnance Survey maps** | Landrangers 92 (Barnard Castle) and 98 (Wensleydale & Upper Wharfedale), Explorer OL30 (Yorkshire Dales – Northern & Central areas) |

*Linking three of Upper Swaledale's delightful villages, this walk, even the longer version, is easy and most agreeable. With the River Swale as a near constant companion, the route explores one of the most outstanding regions of the Dales. This is a walk of magnificent views and great variety embracing riverside meadows, hills, woods, waterfalls and a taste of the Pennine Way long-distance trail.*

The village of Gunnerside dates from the time the dale was settled by the Vikings; its name derives from 'Gunner's saetr', meaning 'Gunner's dwelling place'. In the 19th century, the village was at the epicentre of an important lead mining industry largely concentrated in Gunnerside Gill to the north of the village, which still bears the scars and remains of this industry. Today, it enjoys all the appeal of typical Dales settlements: attractive stone cottages clustered around a village square and from which they radiate; its position just above the Swale is exquisite, perched comfortably amid a complex landscape.

The first part of the walk follows a surfaced lane and makes for speedy and easy progress with lovely views across the dale. Leave the village by setting off along the middle one of three possible lanes branching left from the apex of the bend in the main valley road as it passes through Gunnerside, and follow the lane across the edge of the moors as at first it climbs above the dale, and then steadily descends to the tiny village of Ivelet.

Where the lane meets Shore Gill, it descends to cross it and then rises on the other side to a road junction. Here, bear right, climbing for a while before levelling off and starting to descend to Calvert Houses.

On approaching the first buildings at Calvert, take the track that passes behind them, continuing as the dale starts to change direction a little. Above Rampsholme Farm, the lane ceases to be surfaced, and here two tracks continue forward. Take the right-hand track, and when this forks a short distance farther on, branch left on the more prominent track, now following this as the route heads northwards into upper Swaledale. *Down below, to the left, Rampsholme Bridge spans the river, and anyone preferring to take the shorter option, should here leave the main track and double back down to the bridge – but do not cross it. The return leg, which takes a low-level route past the bridge, is described below.*

Ⓐ Now simply follow the delightful

track up the dale towards the V-shaped ravine of Swinner Gill. The path rises steadily before dropping to cross the gill. Beyond, the track now climbs steeply, passing below delightfully named Crackpot Hall, and soon starting to descend as it races on above the spectacular Kisdon Force to intercept the Pennine Way: a short stretch here is also part of the Northern Coast to Coast Walk, so the bridge spanning the Swale

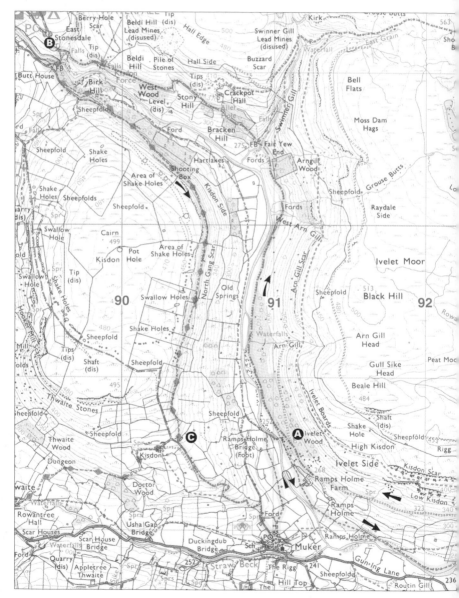

(just before which there are some lovely low waterfalls) is quite a meeting of ways.

**B** Go down to the Swale bridge and climb the rising path on the other side. At the top, turn sharply left to join the southbound Pennine Way, which is now followed across the occasionally rugged flanks of Kisdon Hill.

*River Swale above Muker*

Throughout, the scenery is outstanding and leads to an impressive view over the village of Muker down the length of Swaledale.

At an obvious path junction **C**, bear left onto an enclosed track that zigzags downwards to Muker. On entering the village bear left, and left again at a footpath sign for Gunnerside and Keld, crossing a stone stile and then on a partially paved path across a succession of fields that in spring are bright with buttercups and lead to the bridge spanning the Swale. Cross the bridge and immediately turn right onto a low-level path for Gunnerside. *Here the description for the shorter alternative continues.*

The path leads to a gated gap-stile near a barn beyond which a green track runs across riverside meadows and through more gap stiles (some of them rather narrow) to reach Ivelet Bridge **D**, a lovely, single-arched construction

that lies on the old corpse road linking the upper dale settlements with Grinton, at that time the nearest place with consecrated ground.

From the bridge, walk up into the village and turn right at the telephone box onto a minor road that quickly leads to a gravel path near a cottage on the left and a barn on the right. From a waymark, descend a narrow path on the right to a footbridge spanning Shore Gill. Now another agreeable trail of meadows and stiles leads back to Gunnerside. On the approach to Gunnerside, ignore paths leading down to the riverbank, and branch left instead to a gated gap-stile and a green path across fields back to Gunnerside finally reached through a small estate of stone-built houses. ●

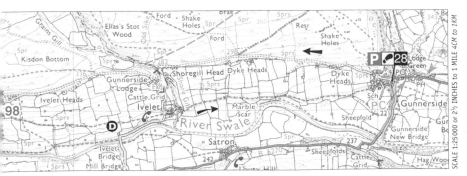

# Further Information

### ■ The National Parks and Countryside Recreation

Ten National Parks were created in England and Wales as a result of an Act of Parliament in 1949. In addition to these, there are numerous specially designated Areas of Outstanding Natural Beauty, Country and Regional Parks, Sites of Special Scientific Interest and picnic areas scattered throughout England, Wales and Scotland, all of which share the twin aims of conservation of the countryside and public accessibility and enjoyment.

John Dower, whose report in 1945 created their framework, defined a National Park as 'an extensive area of beautiful and relatively wild country in which, for the nation's benefit and by appropriate national decision and action, (a) the characteristic landscape beauty is strictly preserved, (b) access and facilities for public open-air enjoyment are amply provided, (c) wildlife and buildings and places of architectural and historic interest are suitably protected, while (d) established farming use is effectively maintained'.

Proposals for the creation of areas of protected countryside were first made before World War I, but nothing was done. The growing demand for access to open country and the reluctance of landowners – particularly those who owned large expanses of uncultivated moorland – to grant it led to a number of ugly incidents, in particular the mass trespass in the Peak District in 1932, when ramblers and gamekeepers came to blows and some trespassers received stiff prison sentences.

It was after World War II that calls for countryside conservation and access came to fruition in parliament. The National Parks and Countryside Act of 1949 provided for the designation and conservation of areas both of great scenic beauty and of particular wildlife and scientific interest throughout Britain. More specifically it provided for the

*The ruins of Easby Abbey*

creation of National Parks in England and Wales. Scotland was excluded because, with greater areas of open space and a smaller population, there were fewer pressures on the Scottish countryside.

A National Parks Commission, a forerunner of the Countryside Commission, was set up, and over the next eight years ten areas were designated as parks; seven in England (Northumberland, Lake District, North York Moors, Yorkshire Dales, Peak District, Exmoor and Dartmoor) and three in Wales (Snowdonia, Brecon Beacons and Pembrokeshire Coast). In 1989 the Norfolk and Suffolk Broads were added to the list. At the same time the Commission was also given the responsibility for designating other smaller areas of high recreational and scenic qualities (Areas of Outstanding Natural Beauty), plus the power to propose and develop long-distance footpaths, now called National Trails.

The authorities who administer the individual National Parks have the very difficult task of reconciling the interests of the people who live and earn their living within them with those of visitors. National Parks are not living museums and there is pressure to exploit the resources of the area, through more intensive farming, or through increased quarrying and forestry, extraction of minerals or the construction of reservoirs.

In the end it all comes down to a question of balance – between conservation and 'sensitive development'. On the one hand there is a responsibility to preserve the natural beauty of the National Parks and to promote their enjoyment by the public, and on the other, the needs and well-being of the people living and working in them have to be borne in mind.

## The National Trust

Anyone who likes visiting places of natural beauty and/or historic interest has cause to be grateful to the National Trust. Without it, many such places would probably have vanished by now.

It was in response to the pressures on the countryside posed by the relentless march of Victorian industrialisation that the trust was set up in 1895. Its founders, inspired by the common goals of protecting and conserving Britain's national heritage and widening public access to it, were Sir Robert Hunter, Octavia Hill and Canon Rawnsley: respectively a solicitor, a social reformer and a clergyman. The latter was particularly influential. As a canon of Carlisle Cathedral and vicar of Crosthwaite (near Keswick), he was concerned about threats to the Lake District and had already been active in protecting footpaths and promoting public access to open countryside. After the flooding of Thirlmere in 1879 to create a large reservoir, he became increasingly convinced that the only effective way to guarantee protection was outright ownership of land.

The purpose of the National Trust is to preserve areas of natural beauty and sites of historic interest by acquisition, holding them in trust for the nation and making them available for public access and enjoyment. Some of its properties have been acquired through purchase, but many have been donated. Nowadays it is not only one of the biggest landowners in the country, but also one of the most active conservation charities, protecting 581,113 acres (253,176 ha) of land, including 555 miles (892km) of coastline, and over 300 historic properties in England, Wales and Northern Ireland. (There is a separate National Trust for Scotland, which was set up in 1931.)

Furthermore, once a piece of land has come under National Trust ownership, it is difficult for its status to be altered. As a result of parliamentary legislation in 1907, the Trust was given the right to declare its property inalienable, so ensuring that in any subsequent dispute it can appeal directly to parliament.

As it works towards its dual aims of conserving areas of attractive countryside and encouraging greater public access (not easy to reconcile in this age of mass tourism), the Trust provides an excellent service for walkers by creating new concessionary paths and waymarked trails, maintaining stiles and foot bridges and combating the ever-increasing problem of footpath erosion.

For details of membership, contact the National Trust at the address on page 95.

## Walkers and the Law

The average walker in a national park or other popular walking area, armed with the appropriate Ordnance Survey map, reinforced perhaps by a guidebook giving detailed walking instructions, is unlikely to run into legal difficulties, but it is useful to know something about the law relating to public rights of way. The right to walk over certain parts of the countryside has developed over a long period, and how such rights came into being is a complex subject, too lengthy to be discussed here. The following comments are intended simply as a helpful guide, backed up by the Countryside Access Charter, a concise summary of walkers' rights and obligations drawn up by the Countryside Commission.

Basically there are two main kinds of public rights of way: footpaths (for walkers only) and bridleways (for walkers, riders on horseback and pedal cyclists). Footpaths and bridleways are shown by broken green lines on Ordnance Survey Explorer maps and broken red lines on Landranger maps. There is also a third category, called byways: chiefly broad tracks (green lanes) or farm roads, which walkers, riders and cyclists have to share, usually only occasionally, with motor vehicles. Many of these public paths have been in existence for hundreds of years and some even originated as prehistoric trackways and have been in constant use for well over 2000 years. Ways known as RUPPs (roads used as public paths) still appear on some maps. The legal definition of such byways is ambiguous and they are gradually being reclassified as footpaths, bridleways or byways.

The term 'right of way' means exactly what it says. It gives right of passage over what, in the vast majority of cases, is private land, and you are required to keep to the line of the path and not stray on to the land on either side. National Park status does not confer automatic right of access. If you inadvertently wander off the right of way – either because of faulty map-reading or because the route is not clearly indicated on the ground – you are technically trespassing and the wisest course is to ask the nearest available person (farmer or fellow walker) to direct you back to the correct route. There are stories about unpleasant confrontations between walkers and farmers at times, but in general most farmers are co-operative when responding to a genuine and polite request for assistance in route-finding.

Obstructions can sometimes be a problem and probably the most common of these is where a path across a field has been ploughed up. It is legal for a farmer to plough up a path provided that he restores it within two weeks, barring exceptionally bad weather. This does not always happen and here the walker is presented with a dilemma: to follow the line of the path, even if this inevitably means treading on crops, or to walk around the edge of the field. The latter course of action often seems the best but this means that you would be trespassing and not keeping to the exact line of the path. In the case of other obstructions which may block a path (illegal fences and locked gates etc), common sense has to be used in order to negotiate them by the easiest method – detour or removal. You should only ever remove as much as is necessary to get through, and if you can easily go round the obstruction without causing any damage, then you should do so. If you have any problems negotiating rights of way, you should report the matter to the rights of way department of the relevant council, which will take action with the landowner concerned, or, in the case of a national park, the relevant national park authority.

Apart from rights of way enshrined by law, there are a number of other paths available to walkers. Permissive or concessionary paths have been created where a landowner has given permission for the public to use a particular route across his land. The main problem with these is that, as they have been granted as a concession, there is no legal right to use them and therefore they can be extinguished at any time. In practice, many of these concessionary routes have been established on land owned either by large public bodies such as the Forestry Commission, or by a private one, such as the National Trust, and as these mainly encourage walkers to use their paths, they are unlikely to be closed unless a change of ownership occurs.

Walkers also have free access to country parks (except where asked to keep away from certain areas for ecological reasons, eg. wildlife protection, woodland regeneration, safeguarding of rare plants etc), canal towpaths and most beaches. You are generally free to walk across the open and uncultivated higher land of mountain, moorland and fell (although not by right), but this varies from area to area and from one season to another – grouse moors, for example, will be out of

*Countryside Access Charter*

*Your rights of way are:*

- public footpaths – on foot only. Sometimes waymarked in yellow
- bridleways – on foot, horseback and pedal cycle. Sometimes waymarked in blue
- byways (usually old roads), most 'roads used as public paths' and, of course, public roads – all traffic has the right of way

Use maps, signs and waymarks to check rights of way. Ordnance Survey Explorer and Landranger maps show most public rights of way

*On rights of way you can:*

- take a pram, pushchair or wheelchair if practicable
- take a dog (on a lead or under close control)
- take a short route round an illegal obstruction or remove it sufficiently to get past

*You have a right to go for recreation to:*

- public parks and open spaces – on foot
- most commons near older towns and cities – on foot and sometimes on horseback
- private land where the owner has a formal agreement with the local authority

*In addition you can use the following by local or established consent, but ask for advice if you are unsure:*

- many areas of open country, such as moorland, fell and coastal areas, especially those in the care of the National Trust, and some commons
- some woods and forests, especially those owned by the Forestry Commission
- country parks and picnic sites
- most beaches
- canal towpaths
- some private paths and tracks Consent sometimes extends to horse-riding and cycling

*For your information:*

- county councils and London boroughs maintain and record rights of way, and register commons
- obstructions, dangerous animals, harassment and misleading signs on rights of way are illegal and you should report them to the county council
- paths across fields can be ploughed, but must normally be reinstated within two weeks
- landowners can require you to leave land to which you have no right of access
- motor vehicles are normally permitted only on roads, byways and some 'roads used as public paths'

bounds during the breeding and shooting seasons and some open areas are used as Ministry of Defence firing ranges, for which reason access will be restricted. In some areas the situation has been clarified as a result of 'access agreements' between the landowners and either the county council or the national park authority, which clearly define when and where you can walk over such open country.

 ## The Ramblers' Association

No organisation works more actively to protect and extend the rights and interests of walkers in the countryside than the Ramblers' Association. Its aims are clear:

to foster a greater knowledge, love and care of the countryside; to assist in the protection and enhancement of public rights of way and areas of natural beauty; to work for greater public access to the countryside; and to encourage more people to take up rambling as a healthy, recreational leisure activity.

It was founded in 1935 when, following the setting up of a National Council of Ramblers' Federations in 1931, a number of federations earlier formed in London, Manchester, the Midlands and elsewhere came together to create a more effective pressure group, to deal with such problems as the disappearance and obstruction of footpaths, the prevention of access to open mountain and moorland

*Further Information*

*The limestone ravine of Trollers Gill*

and growing hostility from landowners. This was the era of the mass trespasses, when there were, at times, violent encounters between ramblers and game-keepers, especially on the moors of the Peak District.

Since then the Ramblers' Association has played an influential role in preserving and developing the national footpath network, supporting the creation of national parks and encouraging the designation and waymarking of long-distance routes.

Freedom to walk in the countryside is precarious and requires constant vigilance. As well as the perennial problems of footpaths being illegally obstructed, disappearing through lack of use or extinguished by housing or road construction, new dangers can spring up at any time.

It is to meet such problems and dangers that the Ramblers' Association exists and represents the interests of all walkers. The address to write to for information on the Ramblers' Association and how to become a member is given on page 95.

 *Safety on the Hills*

The hills, mountains and moorlands of Britain, though of modest height compared with those in many other countries, need to be treated with respect. Friendly and inviting in good weather, they can quickly be transformed into wet, misty, windswept and potentially dangerous areas of wilderness in bad weather. Even on an outwardly fine and settled summer day, conditions can rapidly deteriorate. In winter, of course, the weather can be even more erratic and the hours of daylight are much shorter.

Therefore it is advisable to always take both warm and waterproof clothing, sufficient nourishing food, a hot drink, first-aid kit, torch and whistle. Wear suitable footwear such as strong walking boots or shoes that give a good grip over rocky terrain and on slippery slopes. Try to obtain a local weather forecast and bear it in mind before you start. Do not be afraid to abandon your proposed route and return to your starting point in the event of a sudden and unexpected deterioration in the weather. Do not go alone. Allow enough time to finish the walk well before nightfall.

Most of the walks described in this book do not venture into remote wilderness areas and will be safe to do, given due care and respect, at any time of year in all but the most unreasonable weather. Indeed, a crisp, fine winter day often provides perfect walking conditions, with firm ground underfoot and a clarity that is not possible to achieve in the other seasons of the year. A few walks, however, are suitable only for reasonably fit and experienced hill walkers able to use a compass and should definitely not be tackled by anyone else during the winter months or in bad weather, especially high winds and mist. These are indicated in the general description that precedes each of the walks.

 *Useful Organisations*

**Council for National Parks**
6/7 Barnard Mews, London SW11 1QU
Tel. 020 7924 4077

**The Yorkshire Dales National Park Authority**
Hebden Road, Grassington,
North Yorkshire BD23 5LB
Tel. 01756 752748

Yorebridge House, Bainbridge,
Leyburn, North Yorkshire DL8 3EE
Tel. 01969 650456

*National Park Authority Visitor Centres:*
Aysgarth Falls: 01969 663424
Grassington: 01756 752748
Hawes: 01969 667450
Malham: 01729 830363
Reeth: 01748 884059
Sedbergh: 01539 620125

**Council for the Protection
of Rural England**
128 Southwark Street,
London SE1 0SW
Tel. 020 7981 2800

**Countryside Agency**
John Dower House, Crescent Place,
Cheltenham, Gloucestershire GL50 3RA
Tel. 01242 521381

**Forestry Commission**
Silvan House, 231 Corstorphine Road,
Edinburgh EH12 7AT
Tel. 0131 334 0303

**Long Distance Walkers' Association**
Bank House, High Street, Wrotham,
Sevenoaks, Kent TN15 7AE
Tel. 01732 883705

**National Trust**
*Membership and general enquiries:*
PO Box 39, Warrington WA5 7WD
Tel. 0870 458 4000

*Yorkshire Regional Office:*
Goddards, 27 Tadcaster Road,
Dringhouses, York YO24 1GG
Tel. 01904 702021

**Ordnance Survey**
Romsey Road, Maybush,
Southampton SO16 4GU
Tel. 08456 05 05 05 (Lo-call)

**Ramblers' Association**
2nd Floor, Camelford House,
87-90 Albert Embankment,
London SE1 7TW
Tel. 020 7339 8500

**Yorkshire Tourist Board**
312 Tadcaster Road, York YO24 1GS
Tel. 0870 609 0000

*Local tourist information offices:*
Bedale: 01677 424262
Horton in Ribblesdale: 01729 860333
Ingleton: 015242 41049
Leyburn: 01969 623069
Pateley Bridge: 01423 711147
Sedbergh: 015396 20125
Settle: 01729 825192
Skipton: 01756 792809

**Youth Hostels Association**
Trevelyan House, Dimple Road,
Matlock, Derbyshire DE4 3YH
Tel. 01629 592600 (General enquiries)
www.yha.org.uk

## Ordnance Survey Maps of the Yorkshire Dales

The Yorkshire Dales are covered by
Ordnance Survey 1:50 000 ($1\frac{1}{4}$ inches to
1 mile or 2cm to 1km) scale Landranger
map sheets 92, 97, 98, 99 and 104. These
all-purpose maps are packed with
information to help you explore the area.
Viewpoints, picnic sites, places of interest
and caravan and camping sites are shown,
as well as public rights of way information
such as footpaths and bridleways.

To examine the Yorkshire Dales in more
detail, and especially if you are planning
walks, Explorer maps OL2 (Yorkshire
Dales – Southern & Western areas), OL19
(Howgill Fells & Upper Eden Valley),
OL30 (Yorkshire Dales – Northern &
Central areas) and OL41 (Forest of
Bowland & Ribblesdale) at 1:25 000 ($2\frac{1}{2}$
inches to 1 mile or 4cm to 1km) are ideal.

Other Explorer maps covering the
area are:
298 (Nidderdale)
302 (Northallerton & Thirsk)
304 (Darlington & Richmond)

To get to the Yorkshire Dales, use
Ordnance Survey OS Travel Map-Route
Great Britain at 1:625 000 (1 inch to
10 miles or 4cm to 25km) scale or
Ordnance Survey Road Travel Map 4
(Northern England) at 1:250 000 (1 inch to
4 miles or 1cm to 2.5km) scale.

Ordnance Survey maps and guides are
available from most booksellers, stationers
and newsagents.

*Further Information*

**www.totalwalking.co.uk**
is the official website of the Jarrold
Pathfinder and Short Walks guides. This
interactive website features a wealth of
information for walkers – from the latest
news on route diversions and advice from
professional walkers to product news, free
sample walks and promotional offers.

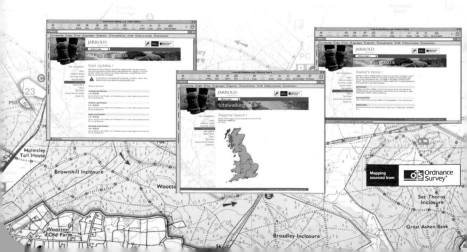